DADBOD

FOCUSING ON **YOU** SO YOU

DAD BOD

ARE THERE **FOR THEM**

JOE WHEELER

COPYRIGHT © 2026 JOE WHEELER

All rights reserved. No part of this book may be reproduced into a retrieval system, or transmitted in any form, or by any means (electronic, mechanical, photocopying, recording, or otherwise) without the prior written consent of the author.

DADBOD

Focusing on You So You Are There for Them

FIRST EDITION

ISBN 978-1-5445-5022-0 *Hardcover*
        978-1-5445-5021-3 *Paperback*
        978-1-5445-5023-7 *Ebook*
        978-1-5445-5080-0 *Audiobook*

LCCN: 2024924733

Disclaimer: Neither the publisher nor the author is engaged in rendering professional advice or services to the individual reader. The ideas, procedures and suggestions contained in this book are not intended as a substitute for consulting with your physician. All matters regarding your health require medical supervision. Neither the author nor the publisher shall be liable or responsible for any loss or damage allegedly arising from any information or suggestion in this book.

The author has done his best to ensure all information provided herein is accurate and up to date regarding Internet addresses, websites, phone numbers, or resources referenced, but cannot be held responsible for any inconsistencies or changes made after book publication.

To my wife and kids, who loved me both with and without my DADBOD

CONTENTS

INTRODUCTION 11

1. THE CURRENT STATE OF THINGS 19
2. HOW'D WE GET HERE? 25
3. MENTAL HEALTH 33
4. RESPECT + ADOLESCENCE = MASCULINITY 47
5. ADOLESCENCE + MASCULINITY = FATHERHOOD 59
6. THE RELATIONSHIP WITH MY PARENTS IS COMPLICATED— WHOSE ISN'T? 65
7. PHYSICAL WELL-BEING 77
8. BE MORE THAN JUST A MIDDLE-AGE TROPE 85
9. MEN'S HEALTH 93
10. THE DADBOD DIET 101

LAST THOUGHT 111
APPENDIX 115
ACKNOWLEDGMENTS 123

|Dadbod|

: A physique regarded as typical of an average father, especially one that is slightly overweight and not extremely muscular.

INTRODUCTION

"Fatherhood is great because you can ruin someone from scratch."
—JON STEWART

Congratulations on being a father! I assume—if it is the title of the book that brought you here—that you are, indeed, a father, or at the very least, a father to be, with a rocking dadbod. As I write this, I do so, fully acknowledging that I am a terrible marketer. I own that I may have successfully alienated over half of the general population. But if you are not a dad yet, or not a dad, period, that is fine too. We all can glean something from connecting with that special father figure in our lives, our husbands, brothers, sons, or even our own dads. Whatever brought you here, it's a privilege to have you.

But let's be real. Being a "father"[1] is, respectfully, not for everyone. This office of fatherhood is uniquely designed to cater to those assigned to the male demographic. Being a dad is inimitable in that you were (hopefully) a system of solid support and a (literally) minuscule contributor[2] to the birthing process and fetal growth of your child until that child was human enough to behold in your arms.

For those of us blessed to experience this, you will agree with me that it is, indeed, one of the most extraordinary and rewarding feelings in the entire world. You have their whole life in front of you and the awesome responsibility of jumpstarting their life and destiny...shaping that human from their starting point. From that pivotal moment, you are not only faced with the opportunity and experience of shaping their destiny; you are choosing yours.

This journey of fatherhood belongs to you. This journey will, undoubtedly, have trials and tribulations, positives and negatives, ups and downs, and at times, it may feel most appropriate to leave your masculinity[3] checked at the door. There will also be times when you perceive the lion of masculinity inside of you, in all its testosterone-laden glory, was born for such a time as this.

All of which brings me to the topic of this book. It's a retrospective of fatherhood and masculinity, so you can balance it all and be the father you want to be—a lens into the modern-day dad through the dadbod.

---

[1] "father: 1a (1) a male parent; 1 a (2): a man who has begotten a child." Merriam-Webster, https://www.merriam-webster.com/dictionary/father. Father sounds so formal—for that reason, I prefer to go by "dad" within my family circle. I fully acknowledge that father comes in many forms: figurative, literal, biological, adoptive, and even religious. What does "father" mean to you? Someone who is there, someone who was not there, someone you relate to, or someone you have nothing in common with, or everything in common with.

[2] The average sperm measures just 4.3 micrometers (μm) long and 2.9 μm wide. https://pmc.ncbi.nlm.nih.gov/articles/PMC3739080.

[3] ...or your societally provoked/endorsed definition of it.

In this book, I'm going to do my best to explore where that masculinity came from, why it may have left, and in some cases, why we should go get it back, and in other instances, permanently let it go. I will use personal stories to share real-life experiences from a dad who is out there just trying to make sense of it all. Then, I will provide some practical tips and tools to set aside preconceived notions, focus your energy where you want to, and start taking real action toward your goals today. I call this a practical approach because so many times, we all know what to do, but for whatever reason, we do not do it. The lessons in this book are designed to be easy to follow to effect small changes in yourself for your benefit. Once that is achieved, everyone around you will share in the benefits.

This, however, is not, in my eyes, a child-rearing book. Do not read this thinking you will get some interesting insight into raising a cool kid—you might not—but that may be the after-effect of being a good dad. However, that isn't the point and purpose of this book. I am a hands-on father who chooses to be an integral part of my kids' daily lives. If you are like me—dads who do enough child-rearing every day—this book is for you, about you, so you are there for them.

But let's get a few things straight: I am not a Navy SEAL, a real-estate mogul, or a billionaire. Although these folks have great stories and experiences to share, it seems like they are mostly trying to sell you on what they did to succeed, or their books are just one-liner quips on ways to be your best self. None of those accolades matter if, at the end of the day, you are not happy or not yourself. I am not them. **I am you**—a basic, normal guy with a job, a wife, and three kids. This book aims to provide insightful clues on how male tropes may have affected you throughout your life; some of these insights may indeed bring some unfulfilled happiness to the forefront. For myself personally, my transformation into fatherhood felt eerily similar to being a teenager again; my thirteen-year-old self—ripe with insecurities, fears, and awareness—directly informed the father I became. So if you feel insecure because you have a dadbod—do not. No one is at fault for your dadbod—and there is nothing wrong with you.

Having a dadbod does not mean you failed in other aspects of your life, and getting rid of your dadbod does not mean you will fail at being a dad. Please go easy on yourself throughout this process. There is one more ask. Please approach this book with a simple can-do attitude and a positive growth mindset. Some requirements and asks of this book require a true and deep commitment to who you are and why you came here in the first place. The challenges may be great—I did it, or at least am trying to—and you can, too. And I guarantee you, if you are a confident man within your mind, body and soul, it will help in being the best father you can be. And that is what matters most.

It took me a lifetime to get to this point. I come from a humble background where there was never enough room, always someone fighting or yelling, and no one was happy. Some of my first memories of childhood are of being so anxious to go to primary school that I would make myself throw up so I could take the day off. My mom worked days, so I stayed home with my Italian grandmother, who smoked like a chimney and watched horror movies on repeat. Somehow, I thought this was a better environment for a young kid than Kindergarten, and no one pushed otherwise.

A story that sums up my early childhood best is when I was kicked out of preschool. Yes, it happens. I clearly remember getting in a fight over glue. I remember being pushed or maybe pushing a kid, but I'm not sure anymore. When the teacher was called about my questionable behavior, my grandmother stormed into that preschool, yelling at the teachers and staff that they let this happen and that I would never be returning to a preschool "like this" again. I never went back to that preschool—or any preschool, for that matter. My childhood was full of these kinds of moments where blame and extremism were normal, and actions and reactions were impulsive and emotionally driven for an immediate and specific outcome without taking into account the larger effect that it had on me.

My grandmother was the matriarch of the entire family; whatever she said was gospel. So, for the men in my life, both my grandfather and father, they usually only watched these memorable, impressionable moments from the sidelines and were not active participants. Perhaps a lesson in absenteeism, or maybe just complacency, not wanting to rock the boat, that would inevitably end in some kind of an argument.

Unfortunately, there was a large chunk of my childhood where my grandmother's unhappiness was palpable everywhere around us, maybe because her life turned out differently than what she had wanted, and her husband, my grandfather, was different from what she wanted. They lived with us my entire childhood, and their unhappiness filtered into the daily lives of my sister and me. Eventually, a long and messy divorce ended their forty-five-year marriage, cancer ended up taking her life too early, and by adolescence, I had lost the one person with whom I had spent most of my life.

For the better part of my childhood, I had the cards stacked against me, but I never let that define me. I come from a rough neighborhood. I attended public schools and had family members who were in and out of institutions. Statistically, I should not be where I am today. Sure, I had help. We all need it—and when we are smart enough to take it, good things can happen, but when I separated myself from the pack, it was with a heightened sense of awareness and self-discipline. The people who know me, really know me, are fascinated by this. It is learned through parts of desperation and survival. I was the kid who never read comic books—I read self-help books. Throughout puberty, I studied Dr. Laura Schlessinger's[4] books more than *Playboy*. I was fascinated by the way people can better themselves—and I wanted to do that, I needed that. I wanted to walk the walk, not just talk the talk. I desired to have character[5] and show others that I did.

Therefore, I was not too distracted by the problems at home. I had a vision of where I wanted to go and how I wanted to be perceived. And these idioms worked. I learned at an early age that moderation is more beneficial than extremism, and yes, you can try or do anything once, but you do not have to, and I was okay with that. They also worked in a practical sense—putting my head down and staying the course allowed me to be the first person to graduate from college in my immediate family and the only person to have an Ivy League degree in my entire family. But you get the point—I rebelled through positive action, whereas my friends went down rabbit holes of addiction.

A few years ago, when I realized I had forgotten a lot of what I had learned and was unhappy with myself, how I looked, and my relationship with my wife and kids, I realized it was time for a change. I needed a shift back to self-discipline and moderation, a chance to reprogram back to finding a way to lead through positivity, and with character and respect.

---

4 Dr. Laura Schlessinger is a marriage and family therapist who wrote thirteen books, with the most famous titled, *Ten Stupid Things Women Do to Mess Up Their Lives*.

5 "character: one of the attributes or features that make up and distinguish an individual." Merriam-Webster.com Dictionary, Merriam-Webster, https://www.merriam-webster.com/dictionary/character. From an early age, I was convinced that character was important. I still think about where it came from for me personally—maybe the idea to please others, to make someone happy, maybe it was just growing up in the 80s, when everything was fueled by optimism and materialism. Where do you think your character came from?

Last but not least, and some minor housekeeping before we dive deeper, each chapter opens with a breakdown of what happened to me over the years and how society may have affected it. It is then accompanied by a MANtra to introduce sub-levels of growth and action items to nail down openness, insightfulness, and improvement. Think of these as "bullet points of action" to be your best self.

I have tried to write this book as openly and honestly as possible. I wrote it for you just as much as I wrote it for myself. Sometimes this book will feel direct, but stick with me. The ideas, thoughts, and concepts in this book are my own, from research, sure, but also from lived experiences. You might read sections of this book that you disagree with, or question, or you want to push back on; please do. I welcome the discussion. Maybe you don't agree with my thoughts on gender (Chapter 2) or that a pull-up is the pinnacle of physical fitness (Chapter 9). That is okay. As a dad of three, I am used to spirited debate and handling disagreements while allowing room for others' opinions.

Oh yes, I write with footnotes. I know, some people hate it, some people love it—others couldn't care less. I'd like to think that the footnotes create a little book within a book, a chance for you and me to go a little bit deeper into an interesting phrase, or a thought process, or a triggered word. When was the last time you said something or thought about something, but asked yourself what it really means to you, or to society as a whole?

Finally, I have nothing extra to sell; nothing left on the table. This would not be a practical guide if I tried to convince you to do something and then sent you to yet another resource or purchase another thing to actually get it. I am an open book, ready to share ideas—take them or leave them. Remember, we got here because we let ourselves, and we can dig ourselves out—and we will. After all, I am just a regular guy with three kids. What do I know?

    Let's go!

Best,
Joe Wheeler

CHAPTER 1

THE CURRENT STATE OF THINGS

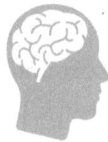

"It is a wise father that knows his own child."
—WILLIAM SHAKESPEARE

Over the last decade, it is safe to say that I have been in the "dad circle"—whether a part of dad groups,[6] parent groups, special nights out, coffee dates, meet-ups, basketball pick-up games, you name it. I have connected with all kinds of dads in all facets and mediums. When you spend a lot of time with a certain subset of people, you notice patterns.

---

6   *Popular Dad Groups:* PEPS: https://www.peps.org/ParentResources/by-topic/just-for-dads. I was a part of this group after my first child was born, did a couple of dad meetings, and found it useful at the time, though I never went back after my first kid. National Fatherhood Initiative—https://www.fatherhood.org/.

Dads kind of look the same—clothing trends froze at about the same time they had kids—so the guy that has the out-of-date wardrobe is probably a dad. Dads wear comfortable, yet somehow cool, shoes at the same time; at least, most of them do. Most dads I know, for whatever reason, use the lower half of their body to home in on a keen fashion sense, and mainly explore shoes—or they wear shorts all of the time and have no fashion sense whatsoever. See for yourself the next time you are around a group of dads. Another obvious trope[7] aside from the kid, diaper bag, and/or stroller in hand is the infamous dadbod.

Sure, some of this can be blamed on aging. The graying and/or loss of hair, the abundance of more hair in the wrong places (think ears, nose, back), and the overall rounding of certain appendages, mainly the mid-section, are all physical factors that have consequently created the modern-day dadbod, and coincidentally, all happen around middle age. We'll discuss more details on this subject in Chapter 8.

I recently read a survey that a higher percentage of women prefer the "dadbod" over a more chiseled and stereotypical male physique.[8] As interesting as this sounds, which is quite a relief for the majority of men, it rings hollow for me.

---

[7] "trope: a common or overused theme or device." Merriam-Webster.com Dictionary, Merriam-Webster, https://www.merriam-webster.com/dictionary/trope. I highlighted this word because it jumped out at me as one to avoid. Especially in our writing, in our speaking, we all try to avoid the "trope"—the overused phrase, the overused word, but somehow we all go back to it. The DADBOD is the ultimate trope—it is easy, it is stale and entirely predictable, and you can spot it coming from a mile away.

[8] Joel T. Wade, "The Unexpected Appeal of Men with Dad Bods," *Psychology Today*, March 27, 2024, https://www.psychologytoday.com/us/blog/the-mate-market/202403/why-do-women-like-men-with-dad-bods.

YOUR AVERAGE JOE

I am married and have three kids. I have a career and a desk job; I work from home, and at the core, I am the quintessential dad—therefore, I am no stranger to the dadbod. But as my dadbod took shape, I noticed other things in my life started to rule and be ruled by the constant reminder that: (1) I had gained weight, (2) I had to decide if I was generally okay with that or not, and (3) my overall confidence and manlihood[9] was affected.

At this stage, we often lose track of certain self-care practices, such as regular gym sessions, a balanced diet, and an active, non-sedentary lifestyle. And the lack of worry over these things, I can only assume, may lean into the new fascination of the dadbod by women. My dadbod says that I am competent enough emotionally to have a wife, and that my wife wanted to procreate with me. Dadbods also say that you do not have certain worries financially; you can afford a posh meal, or several. It also says that I have other things to worry about besides myself—maybe the dadbod is sexy.

In some ways, I mean that; I spent over a decade creating my dadbod. Prior to having kids, my wife and I would cozy up on the couch to watch the latest show on television; then retire to our bedroom, maybe indulge in hot sex, boring sex, or no sex at all. Maybe other things happened, or maybe they did not. But this is where the expectation starts and is set going forward.

If, after having a pint of ice cream on the couch, you get laid, why does anything fitness, health, or wellness matter anymore? The very modern inconvenience of finding a mate is over, so

---

9 "manlihood: the quality or state of being manly (as by having qualities such as strength or virility that are traditionally associated with a man)." Merriam-Webster.com Dictionary, Merriam-Webster, https://www.merriam-webster.com/dictionary/manlihood. I say my "manlihood" was affected because the stereotypical ideas behind this word; strength, courage, power, respect felt lacking—I was not happy with how I felt or looked and therefore everything manly was weakened.

what else is there? There are no more bar hops, getting passed out drunk, wild parties—or, if so, admittedly not that wild anymore. You enter a new phase of life, and with that phase comes a new sense of comfort.

Being comfortable[10] is great most of the time, but when that comfortableness takes over other parts of us, we lose track of what might have been, and in doing so, we lose a piece of ourselves. As your dadbod grew, your confidence more than likely shrank, your blood pressure probably went up, you lost some hair, you probably started buying clothes that were a little baggier than before to hide certain lumps in your figure, and maybe even went up a size or two. You are now more distinguished; you have depth and gravitas.[11]

You are kidding yourself and denying what really happened—you got busy, lazy, and gained some weight. You are not a better man for it, just a heavier one. With the growth of your dadbod, your self-confidence, self-worth, and masculinity shrank.

To be clear, there is no way your wife, co-worker, or random lady at the bar thinks that the dadbod is better than the chiseled, younger-looking man standing next to you. Even so, there is no way that you (and yes, I am speaking to the dad with the bod) feel as relevant, or as confident as the six-pack meathead. But we will get there.[12]

---

[10] "comfortable: affording or enjoying contentment and security." Merriam-Webster.com Dictionary, Merriam-Webster, https://www.merriam-webster.com/dictionary/comfortable. Comfort comes in so many ways—and it is not a bad thing at all, it is a great thing really, especially when that comfort stems from companionship and love. The issue I had was that it made me complacent and lazy.

[11] "gravitas: high seriousness (as in a person's bearing or in the treatment of a subject)." Merriam-Webster.com Dictionary, Merriam-Webster. https://www.merriam-webster.com/dictionary/gravitas. I love this word; it embodies pure masculinity, and I used it purposefully here to make a point. All of us can convince ourselves of something when in reality something else is happening. This is a dangerous path.

[12] If any of the above rang true for you, you are not alone. If some of it seems pointless and you couldn't care less—skip to Chapters 8-10 where we focus on real and practical health tips and advice to focus on the physical things you can do to get your pre-dadbod back.

MANtra

Everything is reversible.

Actionable Items:

- *Everything is reversible,* so my current dadbod is not permanent.
  - Please take at least five minutes to sit in a quiet place—for those of us with kids, this might be in the car before you come home or after the kids leave for school, wherever it is—make sure you're alone. Imagine yourself five years from now. Are you with someone? Are your kids grown? Focus on yourself for the majority of the five minutes. Picture yourself in a way that you can be proud of. Five minutes today to effect change for the next five years is worth it.

- *Everything is reversible,* so I am in charge of how I look.
  - This is a predictable yet surprisingly difficult task. Go to your closet, dresser, wardrobe, or wherever you keep clothes. Pick at least five items that are old, rundown, ugly, the wrong color, you know, those items already in the back of your head—get rid of them. You can do it.

- *Everything is reversible,* so I can choose where I go from here.
  - Make a note, either mentally or handwritten, of one thing that you want to change. This can be as simple as

trying a new cup of coffee, going to bed twenty minutes earlier, spending less time on your phone—pick one thing. Track your success.

CHAPTER 2

HOW'D WE GET HERE?

"The measure of intelligence is the ability to change."
—ALBERT EINSTEIN

Sometime between 2005 and 2008, I saw a television commercial that had a nerdy-looking guy with stereotypical nerd clothes, eyeglasses, mediocre facial hair, unkempt hair—you know the type. Then I saw it again and again. It was the norm for men to be off.

THE HISTORY OF THE DADBOD

Whether ads on television, film, or descriptions in novels, each medium had characters that were nerdy, kind of overweight, and real (ish).

More importantly, it was cool to be slightly less manly. It seemed like everywhere I looked, we were being inundated with metrosexuality[13]—it was cool to have a man bag, have your fingernails and toenails polished, or gain sympathy weight with your wife. Pop culture was slowly emasculating[14] testosterone for the modern man.

Was all of this a maneuver by Hollywood to be more likeable? Or was it a systemic shift based on the way people were already evolving, and what we were watching and reading was just catching up? The ideology is complex—I care more about how it affected me.

I believe a man is a man. There, I said it, and I acknowledge that you may disagree with me. That is fine. I understand there is a societal shift that puts us in a non-binary world where gender is fluid and plurality is celebrated. It's just not the truth that I follow. I believe that the evidence is literally between our legs. So long as we are born with a certain type of genitalia, we live in a binary world. Even so, when this shift started happening, it felt good because I saw myself on television—I felt comfortable, knowing I was represented online or in print. It is easier to accept weight gain if you see it reflected around you.

---

[13] "metrosexual: a usually urban heterosexual male given to enhancing his personal appearance by fastidious grooming, beauty treatments, and fashionable clothes." Merriam-Webster.com Dictionary, Merriam-Webster, https://www.merriam-webster.com/dictionary/metrosexual. This was not necessarily a bad thing—but it was a movement that forced men to think a little bit more about what they were wearing, or how they looked, or their grooming habits.

[14] "emasculate: to deprive one of strength, vigor, or spirit." Merriam-Webster.com Dictionary, Merriam-Webster, https://www.merriam-webster.com/dictionary/emasculate. Everywhere I looked, the focus was shifting, and with that shift away from masculinity, something had to fill the void.

The existing state of things only allowed my dadbod to creep up uninterrupted and without guilt. And worse, this external push allowed my masculinity to slip into a subtle hibernation, so the desire or need to flex my muscles or to hit or kick something, anything—to lift heavy weights, or generally just go to the gym—slowly subsided. So, not only was I personally at a point of comfort, but everything around us said MEN are too much. The combination was the perfect petri dish recipe for less masculinity and more dadbod. The dadbod had become a gateway drug to feminism, and the world was okay with it.

It was 2015 when an article came out that coined the phrase "Dadbod.[15]" It recalled how young women in their early twenties were fascinated by older men who looked real rather than like plastic…they wanted men who had guts rather than six-packs. This came up at the same time we were inundated with the rise of action movies where biceps were bulging, and pecs were bouncing. Of course, the average guy (consequently, the same ones who loved comic book movies) not only appreciated the rise of the dadbod, but also relished the notion that they did not have to look chiseled to be liked.

In the Pacific Northwest, a troubling statistic came to light: Seattle was the fastest-growing city. However, this wave was caused by tech immigration to meet the demand of global companies hiring techies from all over the world. Therefore, the rise in population was primarily driven by mostly nerdy, young men. This was happening in other parts of the country too; smart guys were plentiful and the opposite of the stereotypical man. Rather, a subset of dadbod acceptance was ever more present in areas across the US, with a sudden influx of nerds.

Then, around 2017, a Hollywood insider coined the phrase

---

15   This is the original article that coined the term "dadbod": https://www.theodysseyonline.com/dad-bod.

#MeToo (borrowed from an already existing movement focusing on abuse and women of color) that soon affected every masculine trope that existed. The phrase "man-handled" had a very negative connotation now (maybe rightly so), but it was more so that men and their masculinity now had to seek permission for almost every single action. This was at the same time when consensual contraceptives were made available, and even the idea of a man touching a woman required an extra look, glance, or permission that did not exist prior.[16]

The modern world had a direct assault on masculinity. And as a male husband, and father, these outside forces impacted how I thought about myself and my relationship with my wife.

A very genuine and intimate relationship was now being questioned on how we were supposed to act, even though how we had acted prior was entirely acceptable for us. Having a dadbod leaned into the notion that you are an acceptable man to the universe, *et al*. For all of those reasons mentioned earlier, additionally, the dadbod said you probably respect women, and the weak physique was a free pass from over-masculinity scrutiny. You are a little flabby, so you probably do not abuse women.

Give it another few years (circa 2020), and the term dadbod meant you had to be fit, just not crazy meathead fit—and could still be a dad. It meant that you were supposed to look like those popular A-list actors who have personal trainers, private gyms, meal plans, and millions of dollars at their disposal. Only you had to do it with a kid in your arms, another kid on your neck, all while taking out the trash under quarantine. Realistic expectations went out the window.

---

16   Do you remember when the internet exploded over Keanu Reeves not touching anyone in a photograph? The world applauded his thoughtful actions of respecting women by not touching them, instead putting his arms around them and maintaining six inches of space between his hands and theirs. I'm pretty sure he just didn't want to get sued.

MASCULINITY IS A FOUR-LETTER WORD

Fast forward to where we are today. I walked into a bookstore and asked for some books on masculinity. The sales associate, who was a nice, older lady, said, "Masculinity is a four-letter word now." I kind of nodded, not sure where this conversation was going. She searched for a few seconds in the store database, then looked up at me again and said, "Well, not to me…" We ended up having a nice conversation about history, religion, and society's view toward men, but her message could not have been clearer to me—there is an attack on modern masculinity.

Every other day, there is a new article about a food recall or a new forever chemical found in a hip food alternative. On the flip side, there is also a blip somewhere on overly American citizens with pictures of guns, tattoos, and sunglasses popping up in your feed. The combination has landed us in this over-polarization of right and wrong, good and evil, and men or snowflakes. There is no middle-of-the-road acceptance in anything we do; rather, we find ourselves compensating for something that we feel we lost, or we believe others may have taken away from us. Men today are forced to be masculine and be a douchebag or be normal and be weak. There appears to be no middle ground in accepting that men can experience emotions and express them in a safe and meaningful way. Over-masculinity is now plaguing the US for all of the wrong reasons, and probably in response to the assault on manhood, but doing no favors for an actual cause or change of what is right or emotionally healthy.

Here are three thoughts that might just get me in trouble with certain readers. As I mentioned earlier, I am okay with that. (1) If you carry around a gun because you think it is cool, you are doing it for the wrong reasons. (2) If you disrespect women by not treating them fair, justly, or equitably, you are not a strong man; you are just a chauvinist. And, (3) if you were born with a penis between your legs and use the pronouns "they" and "them" to describe yourself, you might be responding to society's request that you excuse your masculinity from the world; you might even have accepted that your inner strength is not meaningful enough to have impact on yourself and those around you. Let's take this last thought further: changing your pronouns does not mean you are no longer a man; it just means that you do not care enough to be the man to yourself and to others around you.

With these constant dichotomies, at the same time, men are not taking the leap to find a partner or to have kids; heck, men are not even making it out of the basement. Young men in their twenties and thirties find it harder to feel motivated to do just about anything.[17] Why would they if they could sit in a basement surrounded by beta-blockers and not have any accountability to anyone else? This is due to the rise of feminism—yes, there are more females in the world who can do the same things you do and probably do it better than you—but that is not an excuse to not even try to excel or succeed at anything.

The feeling of isolation comes from somewhere—it does not just happen. If you feel isolated, consider stepping into the real world—take a risk, make something happen. You cannot expect to wait for things to happen to you, or when they do, you then complain about how it was the wrong thing or that it did not happen in the exact way you expected.

---

[17] Several years ago, a New York family made headlines when they sued their son to leave the house. The judge sided with the parents, and the thirty-year-old was forced to leave the family home. Apparently, it was because he refused to actually contribute to the household in any way. Three major shifts are happening right now in our society: (1) data shows growing numbers of people living at home longer, (2) it is the worst it has ever been, and (3) it is mostly men.

YOU ARE WHAT YOU EAT

That is enough ideology—men in their forties today are, for the most part, healthy, maybe healthier than their parents were, though there are always outliers. But everyone knows what to eat, what not to eat, how to stay away from certain things that might make you gain weight, and not to over-indulge in processed foods considered generally unhealthy, etc. Over the last few years, we have been inundated with so many food options and subscription packages that we have lost the simplicity of what food health actually is—and when there are too many notes, there is nothing to play.

The modern-day dad does not have the time to research which meal plan is the best for them, which one might work, and which one won't. Because of that, we have what our wives grabbed at the store—processed food that kids love or fast food that is quick and easy. We got to a place where everyone knows what to do, yet no one does it. We are stuck in a state of analysis paralysis where information is plentiful, but useful information is impossible to find. At the end of this book, we will focus on a dedicated meal plan for the working dad that focuses on a high-protein and unique diet combined with important supplements to ensure mental and physical peak performance.

As I wrote in the Introduction, we're the ones who got ourselves here. We can dig ourselves out, and we will.

MANtra

I will be productive and useful.

Actionable Items:

- *I will be productive and useful* for my family.
    - Beta-blockers are creative killers—think Netflix, Facebook, Instagram. When you are spending time on those outlets, you are not bettering yourself or others. Track your screen time and eliminate beta-blockers for thirty minutes a day over the next month. Remove distractions that hinder progress and success in anything that you do.

- *I will be productive and useful* at work.
    - Complete a project you have been working on for too long. We all know which one that is—the project that lingers, does not have an end in sight—the one thing you think about, but for whatever reason, you finish everything else first. Finish it.

- *I will be productive and useful* for myself.
    - If you do not have a hobby, find one. This is crucial in personal development and creativity. You need to think about something other than work and kids. Spend at least one hour a week on your hobby. Make sure your hobby is not a beta-blocker.

―――― **CHAPTER 3** ――――

MENTAL HEALTH

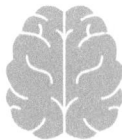

"The people and circumstances around me do not make me what I am, they reveal who I am."
—DR. LAURA SCHLESSINGER

It is imperative that we feel the way we want to, not how we are supposed to. For many years, I resigned myself to the fact that I was overweight, and that my dadbod was distinguished and mature. We all say things to convince ourselves of what we want to hear, even though we know there is only a grain of truth to it. I am a great father, even though I just yelled at my kids and made one of them cry. I'm not overweight, even though my BMI is above normal, and I am pre-diabetic. I love my job, even though I dislike the people I work with and feel that my time is often wasted on busy work.

THE MENTAL HEALTH TRAP

We all fool ourselves into an altered reality. It is not a permanent state, but a mental health trap[18] to make ourselves feel better to avoid the real, hard work of making ourselves better people.

Self-deception is a common process that humans go through to convince themselves of something that is not true to avoid the reality of uncomfortable truths. This manifests itself in a wide variety of ways, but mainly, we rationalize the poor decisions we've made, we do not listen to feedback, or we downplay existing problems as not a big deal, or something we will deal with later.

All of these allow us to continue on a certain path with a certain mindset and be fixed in our ways. This is the antithesis of what actually happens when you are preparing to welcome a new child into your life. Everything changes instantly, and because of that, it is time to face a few common mental health traps that arise for the modern-day dad.

REGRETS

We all have regrets[19]—well, most of us do. I've spent a lifetime trying not to live in the past—but we all do—and have fallen victim to the idea of wanting to do something differently, wishing or hoping that something had a different outcome than

---

[18] "trap: something by which one is caught or stopped unawares, also: a position or situation from which it is difficult or impossible to escape." Merriam-Webster.com Dictionary, Merriam-Webster, https://www.merriam-webster.com/dictionary/trap. I wanted to be specific and deliberate about this chapter because it is an important but often overlooked part of men's health. A trap is a bad thing—a vicious cycle, a downward spiral, something you cannot get out of. We all have them. Acknowledging they exist is our first step in finding our way out.

[19] "regret: to be very sorry for." Merriam-Webster.com Dictionary, Merriam-Webster, https://www.merriam-webster.com/dictionary/regret. I've worked really hard to let regrets go. It is not easy. You cannot control the past; you have to learn and live with it. Make your future worth it.

reality. Naturally, if you wanted something to be different, you might regret not doing something to have made that preconceived outcome a reality.

Regret in the base form means sadness and disappointment—again because you long for a different (usually better) outcome. If we continue to regret our life choices, we will live in a perpetual state of disappointment and sorrow that goes nowhere and ends badly. At the end of the day, there is nothing for it. Being a dad forces many regrets. There are times when you may have acted badly, said the wrong thing, or acted the wrong way. Instead of regretting that moment, learn from it and move on—do not dwell on it because, I guarantee you, your kids already forgot about it. Your wife will forgive you for it, and you will be a better man for letting it go.

No, I am not saying to live carelessly and do whatever the hell you want and not to regret it. That is not living life to the fullest—that is callousness. That life choice is a blatant disregard for those around you, but I am saying that at times, if we feel like we are pushed too far, or maybe lose our tempers or get in an argument, it is okay to do that, firstly, and secondly, it is okay to let it go as well. This misnomer about masculinity, where it is okay to have muscles and testosterone but not okay to raise your voice, is a constant and real dichotomy that the modern-day dad has to contend with. Find a balance and find an outlet, or it will become displaced anger.

DISPLACED ANGER

As men, we are supposed to be kind and thoughtful toward women. At the same time, we're expected to chase sex and "lead with our dicks." Those two expectations don't go hand in hand.

The modern dad has to be able to compartmentalize[20] when it is okay to be a man dad, or a kid dad, or a wife dad. Is it male first, women first, or kid first—because it is nearly impossible to do all of it at the same time with any success? Instead of focusing on what we are supposed to do, we need to re-evaluate how we define masculinity and how our relationship with women affects our relationship with our kids.

In some cases, as a married couple, it may be easier to take out certain emotions toward your partner on your children. This is usually done subconsciously, but frustrations in marriage lead to frustrations with child-rearing and, in turn, short tempers and fuses toward your kids. This happens with every stressor in our lives. It is only exacerbated by your partner because they are your counterpart in child-rearing and the person with whom you may share those stressors.

Here's an example to help you visualize this. The famous movie, *It's a Wonderful Life*,[21] exaggerates this realization of displaced anger all too well. George Bailey comes home to a broken-down house, a sick kid, and another kid pounding incorrect notes on the piano, and rightly loses his cool at the kids and at the schoolteacher when she calls to check up on Zuzu. Obviously, George Bailey did not have an issue with the teacher, but his displaced anger boiled over.

Men have a lot of displaced anger, and when we generally do not have a means to let out that aggression, it comes out in

---

20 "compartmentalize: to separate into isolated categories." Merriam-Webster.com Dictionary, Merriam-Webster, https://www.merriam-webster.com/dictionary/compartmentalize. I think men, especially, are better at doing this. We will not discuss something important or hold something back, as opposed to our lady counterparts, who may need to talk it out or communicate exactly what they are thinking. As men, we may have something to learn from others: instead of holding everything in, we could try sharing more.

21 *It's a Wonderful Life*. Dir. Frank Capra. Perf. James Stewart, Donna Reed, Lionel Barrymore, and Thomas Mitchell. RKO, 1946.

other forms, usually at our partners or kids. I do not recommend that we entirely forget we are men; rather, we need to give ourselves the proper means and channels to exude some form of testosterone out of the home in a safe and logical manner. Whether working out, playing a sport, or working around the house, doing something physical is necessary.

I had a lot of anger when I was a kid. I remember we had a sunset room that was half outside and half inside, and some pipes went through it. I was around ten years old or so, and I just could not take the bottled-up anger anymore, so I kicked the pipe. It exploded and water went everywhere. My mother kept asking, "Why did you kick the pipe?" All I could do was shrug. I still do not know to this day why I kicked that pipe, but I could not control myself, my anger, my bodily motor skills—nothing made sense.

Growing up, I eventually found another outlet for my anger; I played baseball, and I started pitching. I was pretty good and practiced all the time. In our yard, we had a wide brick concrete wall on one side where I drew a black circle, counted the steps off, and threw a baseball for hours at a time. This was cathartic for me—no matter what was happening around me, I had an outlet to wind up and throw a ball as hard as I could toward a brick wall. Day after day, I would do that.

We went on to win baseball games, and won the local Little League championship that year, but none of that mattered—I had a baseball and a wall. Then one day, I threw the ball right on the spot, and it went through the concrete fence—I had broken a concrete brick wall with a baseball. I guess I needed another outlet.

My advice about displaced anger: find something, anything to bear the brunt of it that's far apart from your wife and kids. They do not deserve it—they just happen to be sharing space with you. Take out your anger on some physical activity, so you don't take it out on those closest to you.

ADJUST YOUR THINKING

The power of positive thinking—what a joke! That phrase is such a cliché now and a term of art that it has lost any real meaning. If you think positively, positive things will happen to you. Norman Peale coined the phrase with his 1952 Self-Help book, *The Power of Positive Thinking*, and in that book is a step-by-step guide on how to clear your mind, think positively, and good things will happen to you. With the help of God, and of course, your patience and fortitude, it will happen.

Over the years, what the power of positive thinking does not highlight is that it takes thoughtful thinking to understand what is positive and what is negative, and to whom. If you sat and meditated every day and decided that you wanted to be rich, you may start to formulate a plan. This plan may involve long hours, dabble in borderline criminal activity or pyramid schemes, get-rich-fast scams, might afford you a willingness to take risks with your investments, or do something rash—but you are positively moving toward your singular goal. It is positive to have money and to think about ways to get there.

However, positive does not mean accurate. The power of positive thinking only works if it comes from a place of pure positivity with a positive goal in mind, with a positive outcome—otherwise, the premise fails miserably. Instead, we should think of our thinking as a thoughtful tool to effect change, not as a superpower to give us what we want in life.

When I was sixteen years old, I had a "girlfriend"—it was the first time I had a serious relationship and the first person I fell in love with—if you can do that at sixteen. Like any first love, it ended too fast, with lots of drama and broken hearts. I remember having such deep, strong emotions at that time that I had a hard time getting over the break-up, the change, the failures, the loss, whatever it was—high school, right?

I was grasping at anything to get over the relationship, and this power of positive thinking came back to me. I'm sure I read it prior (I wasn't kidding when I said I read lots of self-help books), and I decided to try the tools to adjust my thinking on the relationship differently. It did not work. Instead, I approached the thinking differently. I thought about a way that it might make me feel better, and that was to put all of those emotions into a mental box and drop that box into a dark void.

I remember sitting in my room in the dark and picturing images of my ex-girlfriend and dropping them in an abyss of darkness—never to be seen again. I did this over and over again. I'm sure this mental health strategy exists somewhere in the world; I probably did not create it, but I did utilize it. And when I had reached a point of comfort, I had come out on the other side freer of my thoughts, anxieties, worries, failures, and misgivings. She had moved away, out of state, shortly after our break-up, and when she came to visit some friends at my high school graduation, we connected briefly, shared a nice conversation, and went our separate ways.

I remember I did not have a lot of feelings either way, and my thinking at the time was that maybe my mental abyss actually worked.

We have the ability to think positively, and think negatively, let emotions take us over, think happy thoughts or not, but the most important thing is that we can control our thoughts and what we think about them.

That's what I realized when I was sixteen: that the power of positive thinking is that you are what you think. At sixteen, did I mentally put my ex-girlfriend in a dark abyss somewhere to better cope with my emotions? Yes, but in doing so, I coped with my emotions. I took the steps to think through what that looked like and to imagine myself without her. She did not go anywhere; her mental hold over me did—and that's what mattered.

As men, fathers, husbands, and partners, we face challenging situations that we face on a daily basis. Take the mental breaks you need to flesh out strong emotions in a positive way.

PERINATAL DEPRESSION

Men experience perinatal depression[22] at an alarming rate. The National Institute of Health has found that fifteen percent of men experience some kind of anxiety or depression in the anticipation of having a child.

Furthermore, men experience postpartum depression in very similar ways that women do—and it is only at a slightly reduced percentage. However, you would never guess that based on the societal norms that the men are supposed to stay strong, and the women can emote. As the preparation for a new baby comes, so does the anticipation and anxiety that a new person is joining your family. This embodies itself in extra weight gain (for women, they have an excuse; for men, it is a different ball game altogether).

It always floored me that there was a craze where it was cool for men to gain sympathy weight so they could be more like their female counterparts. This process was so cool it got a

---

22 "depression: a state of feeling sad." Merriam-Webster.com Dictionary, Merriam-Webster, https://www.merriam-webster.com/dictionary/depression. I felt like a failure. I struggled with this, but for me it was the idea of not living up to my potential, and letting myself go—it comes in many forms, and many times it is exacerbated by our actions, counterintuitively we do not help ourselves, we let ourselves go.

name called Couvade Syndrome,[23] when partners experience symptoms of pregnancy, similar to their pregnant counterpart during pregnancy, and comes in the form of weight gain, nausea, stress, and emotional anxiety. No shit—it's called life. If your partner is experiencing those things, of course, you are too. Everyone in the same house would be—that is life, that is what being a partner is all about—to share emotional highs and lows, to experience things together. This is not a syndrome.

After having three kids, I can tell you wholeheartedly I never wanted to be pregnant—or experience a pregnancy. My wife is a superhero for what she did and how she did it—she made three beautiful kids and had three natural childbirths, one even at home on a couch. I gained some weight, had some highs and lows, but it is not the same thing.

Dads have no right to gain weight and then blame their pregnant wives for it—or to call it a syndrome. If this is you, stop it.

THE BLAME GAME

Speaking of blame,[24] how many times have we pointed the finger at others instead of at ourselves? It is so common to do this, and much easier to do so in a tense situation. We may blame someone else for something bad that happened, for a shortcoming, or for not doing something differently. At the

---

23 Here is an interesting article on Couvade Syndrome, https://www.healthline.com/health/pregnancy/couvade-syndrome. I chose this article to include here because it outlines what this is but also has a few practical tips on how to handle it. I personally did not experience this, and I know my opinions on this subject are strong.

24 "blame: to hold responsible for." Merriam-Webster.com Dictionary, Merriam-Webster, https://www.merriam-webster.com/dictionary/blame. I feel like this was always an issue in my house growing up—there were always winners, therefore there was a loser, and with that, the blame that something happened because of you, or did not happen because of your inaction. I worked hard over the years to not think like this—it is a vicious cycle that gets you nowhere.

MENTAL HEALTH · 41

end of the day, this behavior is associated with a serious lack of personal accountability and is entirely fixable. You may be saying to yourself right now, "I do not do that." Well, that is another example of blame without awareness; it's called blame without reflection.

Kids are no strangers to the blame game. Kids always point the finger at someone else. To me, this makes sense; they do not have years of experience telling them that there is another way—so, when they fall down and skin their knee, and someone is standing next to them, the first reaction is to associate that pain with someone else and react. Period. That is all that happened—a very visceral[25] and common action and reaction. When that goes unchecked for the better part of your life, you have a problem.

Remember how I read self-help books on repeat—one book that stuck with me from my adolescence was *Zen in the Art of Archery*.[26] The thesis of the book is that human behavior is learned, and our unconscious and conscious actions are born through repetitive and constant motions, setting up our minds and bodies to be in sync—how an archer pulls back the bow and aims.

There is an awareness of self that requires your mind to get out of the way and let your body do what it is trained to do. When I read this book, my largest takeaway at a young age was that behaviors are learned. All behaviors. So, if we learned to blame someone, we would continue to do it over and over again, until it becomes second nature—the antithesis of course, is not to blame, but rather reflect and account—a much harder thing

---

[25] "visceral: dealing with crude or elemental emotions." Merriam-Webster.com Dictionary, Merriam-Webster, https://www.merriam-webster.com/dictionary/visceral. I love this word—it is so poignant. I used it here because the raw emotion from kids sometimes is preciously visceral.

[26] Eugen Herrigel, *Zen in the Art of Archery*, Translated by R. F. C. Hull (Pantheon Books, 1953).

to do. Next time you want to blame someone, take a beat, ask yourself a very simple question: "What did I do in this situation?"

Let's go back to perinatal depression for a moment. Men must acknowledge the very real fact that their partners go through a huge physical and emotional transformation during pregnancy that makes them not want to have sex. This is nothing personal against you or what you did—it is not about you at all. You are the after-effect of the larger journey of what is happening in your family—the addition of another human being.

Now, flip the switch. Imagine you gained an extra thirty pounds in a pretty quick span, never really felt like yourself, and were bloated and gassy all the time. Would you want to have sex? Well, maybe—but admittedly, you probably would not enjoy it that much. Even so, throughout this time, it is imperative to keep an open communication going about the needs and wants of you and your partner.

Continuing an emotional and physical connection is crucial in your relationship, and the worst thing you can do is start to crack your relationship over bullshit right before a baby comes. I have seen this happen over and over again with friends and colleagues of all ages. Be open and honest with your partner about physical and emotional needs throughout the childbearing process, and no one will be resentful.

POSTPARTUM DEPRESSION

One in ten men experiences some form of postpartum depression. When men become dads, much like when women become mothers, a lot of shit changes in a pretty short time. After the baby is born, you do not sleep very well (if at all), you have added stressors coming from every direction, and there is a required amount of time that you have to wait to have sex.

In addition, your partner probably does not want to do anything else fun or interesting in the bedroom during this time since everything is singularly focused on your new baby—as it should be. Some men experience this and frankly do not have the emotional depth to process it all—and rightly so. There is nothing quite like becoming a father.

Starting a new job, going away for college, moving out of state, traveling abroad...nothing quite compares to adding a dependent to your life—for the rest of your life. Nothing is temporary anymore, and everything is plural now. If you have multiple kids, plurality has a new meaning, and there may always be a kid with you. That is the story in my house, as we have three kids, so at least one is always with either my wife or me. It is a rare moment that either one of us is alone, or both of us are alone together.

Throughout all of this change, men can get depressed, but our depression comes out differently than women's, and usually shows up in the form of anger, shortness, irritability, and more risk-taking behaviors (more alcohol, substance abuse issues, reckless driving, pushing boundaries online, extreme sports or violence, and maybe even an affair).

As we work through the rest of this book, it is imperative to approach and acknowledge your current mental state. It is healthy and normal to have insecurities; it is only when those insecurities take over everything we do that we really suffer and possibly cause others around us to suffer. As important as acknowledging the mental health trap exists, we must also know when it takes over.

If you feel like you're deep in a mental health situation right now, please seek the appropriate professional guidance beyond this book. If you are like me, where you had a gnawing sense that you were off and maybe could be or do better, wrapped up in self-deception where nothing was actually a problem, even though everything kind of was, I would suggest starting to work through the action items below. Break free of the mental health trap. Stop convincing yourself you are good and actually make yourself good. It's worth it.

MANtra

Be the man you aspire to be today.

Actionable Items:

- *Be the man you aspire to be today* so that your wife appreciates you.
  - Do one extra thing around the house without being told to do it. We all know what these things are—taking out the trash, loading/unloading the dishwasher, stopping by the grocery store to pick up a few items you need. You already know what it is—go and do it. Do not seek acknowledgement or approval, just do it.

- *Be the man you aspire to be today* so that your kids admire you.
  - Spend meaningful time with your kids by meeting them at their level. If your kids are older, be a true sounding board and listen intently to what they have to say; if they are younger, encourage them to show you a toy they like and explain everything it does. Give 100 percent of your attention when you're with them.

- *Be the man you aspire to be today* so that your colleagues respect you.
  - Ask a friend, co-worker, or colleague if you can help them with something. This may be a project, yard work, helping with a move, or picking up a few cases. Even the simple ask shows that you are a team player and someone they can trust.

CHAPTER 4

RESPECT + ADOLESCENCE = MASCULINITY

"Adolescence represents an inner emotional upheaval, a struggle between the eternal human wish to cling to the past and the equally powerful wish to get on with the future."
—LOUISE J. KAPLAN

I always thought of respect[27] as something that kind of just happens to us. It took me many years to figure out that respect is earned, given, and taken away—that our actions and

---

[27] "respect: to be considered worthy of high regard." Merriam-Webster.com Dictionary, Merriam-Webster, https://www.merriam-webster.com/dictionary/respect. I wrote in detail how important this word is throughout this chapter—you really need to understand what it means to you. For me, it was the catalyst that created my character.

reactions define it, and what we do and how we treat others actually matter.

Growing up, I always wanted to be respected. From a young age, you learn about scholars, businessmen, doctors, and lawyers, and you develop these preconceived notions of what it means to be successful.

My public school education was nothing special, but I remember how we focused on a unique inventor or entrepreneur throughout grade school and learned about their innovations that changed the world. From Edison and the light bulb to Graham Bell and the telephone, the list is endless. Each time there was a distinguished picture, and a staunch-looking fellow who accomplished something. We were expected to respect these people, but what earned that respect—that they accomplished something, or that we talked about it? It had to be both because one would not exist without the other.

Further, respect is an introspective opinion of how we perceive ourselves in the world and how we interact with others. You've likely heard this before: if you do not respect yourself, no one will respect you. So how do you respect yourself? It is all about self-confidence, and what you put out into the world will come back to you. If you take action, show assertiveness, speak clearly, and stand up straight, these are all physical attributes that earn respect. Think of the antithesis to this—someone who is maybe uninterested, not engaging, and dresses poorly. Our first instinct is not respect, but rather the assumption that the person is not doing well, or not in a good place. Take the handshake, for example.

THE HANDSHAKE

One of the most crucial moments for men is the initial meeting, often marked by a handshake. Think of the first time dogs meet, there is a lot of posturing and sniffing, etc. Men are no different, and you should think of the handshake in the same way that two dogs sniff each other's butts. The handshake is a bit more civilized, but it achieves the same purpose—at the end of it, you ultimately know what kind of person you are dealing with, and whether you can and should respect them.

I'm a business professional, and as such, I have extensive experience with handshakes. I have experienced them all: the awkward hold, the firm grip, the weak grip, the half grip, and the finger grip. We'll go through all of these in turn.

First, you never want to be the one with the weak handshake. It is far better for the other person to think, "This guy has a strong handshake," rather than the opposite. If they comment on it, that would be even better. I was always one of the younger guys throughout my career. Starting in sales, I worked with senior execs, who were always older than I was. Because of this, I always had a "junior mentality," but I had a killer handshake, and everyone commented on it. There is no better first impression than a strong handshake.

On the other hand, a weak, feeble, or limp handshake signals timidity, shyness, or disinterest. And combined with no eye contact—forget it. Whatever you're doing is not going anywhere. It is also vital to remember that it takes two to complete a handshake. Whether we like it or not, there are immediate, simultaneous reactions—visceral, physical, mental, and emotional—happening all at once. Maybe it is human interaction, or just our more primal instincts—whatever it is, it exists, and it is real.

Sometimes, handshakes can go a little off, often due to a

misalignment that results in a half grip. When this happens, it is best to start over rather than finish the half grip. If you do not, you are left with a half-read impression of the person and the situation—and no one wants that.

I recall a business setting when we were meeting a client's attorney for the first time. The attorney was soft spoken, and his handshake stood out because he only gripped the fingers, giving more of a finger grip than a full handshake. This was particularly striking to most of us, to the point that we all commented on it after the meeting. We then proceeded to railroad the client's wishes, having lost respect for both his counsel and him due to the overly limp handshake.

Sometimes, handshakes start off great but end up a little awkward. I was meeting with my boss's boss for the first time, and based on my work and feedback, we were both excited to meet. The initial handshake and the meeting were great, but when we went in for a closing handshake, it turned into a weird combination of a shake, a grip, and an awkward hand slide—it was kind of comical. I mention it now because it still astounds me how something so small and seemingly trivial can have such a huge impact on our psyche and our relationships going forward.

Use the handshake as a simple reminder that respect is earned. Do not overlook the little things we do, as they can have a huge impact on how we are respected, perceived, and how others see us. Small, trivial, and mundane yet respectful actions may affect how a deal is shaped, how you meet your wife, or how your kids view the world.

RESPECT + ADOLESCENCE

All of these opinions and feelings about our self-worth start at an early age, and begin to define us in adolescence—that unique time when we transition to adulthood. Most people experience rapid growth and development physically, mentally, and emotionally. At this time, we form certain behaviors that construct the rest of our lives.

We all go through this phase, and probably have funny, horror, or even both types of stories about it. Whatever those stories may be, they certainly shaped us into who we are today. Adolescence, for most boys, is awkward. It was especially awkward for me. I was always good at sports, but I also put on a lot of weight very fast. This dichotomy did not make any sense because I was incredibly active, yet very chubby at the same time. At a time in my life when I had coaches and supporters pushing me to excel in the sport I loved, I found myself distracted by how my shirt hung or revealed my wobbly bits, worried that people were watching that instead of the game. Physical insecurity started to take over my mental awareness, and not in a healthy way.

Of course, this is the first time that I started to notice girls as well, which made for another complication I was not prepared for at the time.

On the way home from a middle school tennis match, we all piled into the school van and started the drive back. It was getting dark, and I sat in the back of the van beside Bethany, a beautiful girl with fair skin and long black hair. She leaned in and tried to kiss me, catching me off guard. When she tried again, I pushed her away. She persisted, but eventually, my strength overpowered her, and it became clear that nothing was going to happen—at least not the way she envisioned it.

The very real truth came out at that singular moment—I was

not ready. I was not ready to kiss a girl, or to have a girl think of me in that way. I was aware that I did not feel like a man yet; for whatever reason, I did not want to kiss her or have her kiss me. Was I gay? No, I had no idea why my reaction was so visceral, but the more I thought about it, the more I realized that I did not feel like I deserved to be kissed, not that I did not want to kiss her or be kissed.

Always remember that how we perceive ourselves and how others perceive us are two very different things. I did not want respect because I did not have it for myself—I was too awkward to feel self-confident enough to be liked.

I carried this weight of uncertainty around for several years. I started to feel bad and awkward about myself. I often wondered if anyone liked me and felt conscious that I looked a certain way. Between the ages of twelve to fifteen, I was kind of a mess—we all were. Around this time, I remember having my first crush on a girl as well—and that is nothing special, but I share it here because, at the end of the day, I think it is a direct reflection of respect for oneself and others.

This girl was the dream girl; she was tall, blond, and the church-going type, the kind of girl a young dork dreams of. I was overweight, awkward, and goofy. There was never a chance.

Meeting in middle school, I kind of assumed that everything would change in high school. I went to a magnet school for the arts, so I had to audition to get into the school. I was sure I would not know anyone if I actually got the chance to attend. Fast forward to the first day of high school, and my crush walked into my homeroom.

I was floored; that was not supposed to happen. As high school went on, I often fantasized about what could be, and as the years went on, I slimmed down, got kind of popular, and actually asked this girl out to our senior prom. She agreed and we went together. I finally respected myself enough to take a risk—my self-confidence existed, I respected myself, and she knew it.

There was nothing more beyond that—there didn't have to be. I do remember reconnecting with her years later after we were both broken and beaten down from bad relationships. We talked all night, shared stories, and eventually went our separate ways. I hope I earned her respect.

EXPECTATIONS

During adolescence, there are a lot of firsts, and those firsts shape the men we become. The first kiss, the first orgasm, the first crush, the first hairs—each of these rites of passage paved the way for the modern-day dad's masculinity and created a pre-defined societal expectation of how a man is supposed to act rather than how a person does act.

In my adolescence, I had masculine tropes forced upon me in everything I did. I was supposed to look a certain way, act a certain way, be a certain way—masculine. You are supposed to be the strong person, the rock, the person who has their shit together because others do not. These expectations force men to rise up or buckle under the pressure. The only way I survived is that I approached everything in moderation.

I was the kid who drove everyone home after an experimental binge, and this allowed those around me to respect me and my self-discipline. They saw in me a protector, a kind of father figure, and a leader to my peers, but not because I led. I handled each situation with dignity and respect, and I protected those around me. In adolescence, we start to shape the type of father we will become.

Those friends of mine who went crazy and partied are the

same dads who still have boys' night out—or get blacked out drunk at football games. Who we were matters because ultimately, it is who we became.

There are certain moments in your life where you see your life flash before your eyes, and after they happen, you start to view things differently. I was not driving yet, so I must have been around twelve or thirteen years old, and a family member and I were driving an ATV in the woods. I lost control of the vehicle and slammed into a giant redwood tree. The ATV flipped with us on it, we were thrown off, and the vehicle landed on top of us. I shimmied out, lifted the ATV off my cousin with strength that I did not know I possessed, and saw things differently from that point forward.

You can be the person people respect, or you can cower in fear when adversity happens. That day, we were lucky, no broken bones, just broken egos, but lessons learned that lasted a lifetime—be the person who lifts others up rather than beats them down.

This continues on to this day in everything that I do, in my work and in my relationships with my wife and kids. Be the person who earns respect by leading with a reckless disregard for doing the right thing—I realized this in my adolescence, and that has led to a life of earning the respect of those around me. For this reason, my masculinity has never faltered.

That is what we must do—earn each other's respect. And this is no different for our colleagues, partners, wives, and kids. Our kids do not want a parent who doesn't deserve respect; they demand it in everything we do, and your kids will push you for it—it is up to us to show them what it is, how to create it, and how to earn it.

My wife and I always go back and forth on this. She wants to be best friends with my kids, and she is, but at times, my kids have a hard time seeing her as anything other than that—and she knows there have been times when they did not respect her. On the flip side, there have been times in my life when my kids may have feared rather than respected me, and the difference is palpable.

As dads, we need to strike a balance of respecting ourselves to ensure that those around us respect us. This is done through thoughtful consideration of everyone's feelings, valuing opinions, listening intently, and creating a fair and equal playing field. My kids have a sense of equity in our home where everyone has a voice—and this has fostered an environment of respect for each other that my kids will take with them for a lifetime.

If they know their opinion matters, they know they can express it freely and confidently because what they say has value. They have self-confidence I never had, and I showed them how to get there. You have the same ability as a dad to shape that confidence by showing your kids their voice matters.

MANtra

I respect myself.

Actionable Items:

- *I respect myself* because I have self-confidence.
  - In order to respect ourselves, we need to be confident in who we are. Practice a calm assertiveness to ensure you are respected by thinking about how you would speak confidently in a business setting. Picture yourself in a situation where you feel undervalued or disrespected and flip the switch—imagine being brave, bold, and assertive.

- *I respect myself* because I respect others.
  - We must exude respect in order to receive it. By sharing with others that you admire certain traits or abilities, you are earning respect by exposing yourself. Let someone know that you admired their ability to overcome a recent challenge or adversity. By telling this person you admire them, they will think differently of you.

- *I respect myself* because I create a space of equity and inclusion.
  - In our daily lives, try to foster a culture of unity and collaboration by asking for everyone's opinion. This can be something as simple as making sure the person who

does not speak up gets the final word or makes the final decision. This can be anything, like which movie to watch or what to make for dinner. Give a voice to someone who doesn't generally use theirs.

CHAPTER 5

ADOLESCENCE + MASCULINITY = FATHERHOOD

"The ability to be in the present moment is a major component of mental wellness."
—ABRAHAM MASLOW

The chapter title is not meant to be derisive[28]—it is a simple fact.[29] For argument's sake, if one of the most "masculine" things you can do is to have sex—that's all you want to do at

---

[28] "derisive: expressing or causing contemptuous ridicule or scorn." Merriam-Webster.com Dictionary, Merriam-Webster, https://www.merriam-webster.com/dictionary/derisive.

[29] I warned you up front that there are some concepts and ideas in this book you may disagree with. Again, it's okay if you do.

a certain point in your life—and that leads to impregnating a woman, then adolescence + masculinity = fatherhood.

In the previous chapter, we explored adolescence in depth, and how this pivotal phase shapes the kind of man we become—whether for better or worse.

Fast forward ten, fifteen, or twenty years, and we are about to welcome our first child. In response to this, our emotional selves and awareness heighten, and hormonal changes in our wives lead us to follow suit.[30] We gain weight at an alarming pace to catch up with wives who are having babies, and within the span of a year, we have almost entirely transformed into a different person. Sound familiar?

The same thing that happens during puberty happens around the beginning of fatherhood. It took me a long time to realize this, and some men never make this cognitive leap. For those of us who embrace this part of our journey, it is satisfying knowing what it is all in preparation for. However, for certain men, this adjustment or shift never actually happens. These men are stuck somewhere in full manhood without embracing what fatherhood has the potential to become, like a raucous teenager who never grows up.

What happens next, after childbirth, is probably the most important piece to the next phase of your life. Did you step up, or run away—are you physically, mentally, and emotionally available, or do you still play mental and emotional games with your partner, kids, or loved ones? Did you get crushed by an ATV, or did you lift it up?

That answer may vary from day to day, month to month,

---

30   I personally gained about twenty-five pounds when my wife went through her first pregnancy. I then gained another ten pounds with my second child and another ten pounds with my third child. Over the course of about eleven years, I gained a lot of "sympathy" weight (forty-five pounds).

or year to year—fatherhood and all of the aspects of it are complicated—and that is okay. And be prepared because it lasts a lifetime. If you are in a monogamous relationship and sharing these experiences with your partner, the rewards could not be greater, and the challenges could not be more real. A central support system is crucial throughout the personal growth and development process. Almost anything is impossible to do within a silo—the best success comes from both internal reflection and external reinforcement.

BEING PRESENT

If my children have taught me anything, it is that being present is a simple way to live your life. So often, we are bogged down by what happened prior or what is going to happen in the future. Why? We have no control over those things—we can only control what is in front of us and what we have to do next.

Children know this. It is only after they grow up that we re-tune them to think ahead, make goals, and make choices about a future they have no interest in leaning into today. And for young kids, that pure desire to only think about what is in front of them is a gift—a gift that we can all learn from.

Fatherhood is no different—it is about being present in your child's life. Being a dad comes with certain challenges. My wife was part of a moms group back in the day, and there was a lady who was a part of that group who spent all of her time complaining that she does ninety-nine percent of child rearing because her husband works all of the time. She was forever known as "99% Mom" in our household.

This woman was resentful, the father was non-existent, and the sentiment was palpable—and this was all because they were stuck in a rat race of stereotypes where the man worked, and the woman raised kids. If this is you, try the tools I give you to open yourself up to those around you, to being present when the time is there. Be around on weekends, show up after work or at an after-school event—be as present as you can, all things considered. Be the best hard-working dad you can be—your wife will not resent you for it.

For those men who read this book and do ninety-nine percent of the child rearing, I salute you. I had a family friend who quit his job to be with the kids. After six months, he was back to work—and it wasn't that he could not handle it. I think he could, but ultimately, he did not want to. He didn't want to always be focused on a kid's needs, warming a bottle, changing a diaper, or having a little kid yell at him over putting on the wrong sock. He knew his limitations and made an adjustment. The family is happier for it.

CHECKMARK-MAN

And that is what I am getting at with all of this "adolescence + masculinity = fatherhood" because the growth process defines what kind of man you are. Are you that person who has poured everything into something else as an excuse to actually not have to spend time with their family, never embracing fatherhood, but stuck in manhood? I call this the "Checkmark-Man."

This guy did everything he was supposed to do and crossed it off the list—college, check; marriage, check; family, check—but never actually wanted any of it, and never wanted to take the next step of personal growth and development to be a parent. Now he pours himself into every other thing there is other than the most important thing—his family.

On the flip side, I worked with a guy who had four kids and was down-to-earth and pretty pragmatic about fatherhood.

You got the sense that he was in it for the long haul and had a good relationship with his kids. I know this because he always made a joke when anyone ever commented on how many kids he had. He'd always say, "I'm just in it for the sex." Everyone in the room would laugh, but when I actually talked to him one-on-one, he knew everything about his kids on a level I can only hope I can communicate to others. This was a guy who had found that balance of fatherhood and masculinity by which we can all aspire to. Again, it all comes down to sex.[31]

---

[31] That was a joke.

MANtra

Adolescence + Masculinity = Fatherhood

Actionable Items:

- *Adolescence + Masculinity = Fatherhood* because I wanted to be a dad and chose to have a family.
    - Regardless of the situation, it is likely that, if you are reading this book, you can say "Yes" to the statement above. Repeat it several times a day until you believe it. If you did not choose to be a dad or to have a family, and you still have one, you are choosing to stay around.

- *Adolescence + Masculinity = Fatherhood* because I am proud to be a dad.
    - Tell your kids you are proud of them for something they accomplished. Just recounting that sentence makes you automatically think of something that you are proud of or not proud of. Whichever it is, be proud.

- *Adolescence + Masculinity = Fatherhood* because I am a dad.
    - If you are a male dad and you have a kid, there is a certain equivalent that in fact you are masculine, regardless of how you look, what you wear, or what you feel. If there is nothing to be proud of in the previous affirmation, be resolved and be proud in that.

CHAPTER 6

THE RELATIONSHIP WITH MY PARENTS IS COMPLICATED— WHOSE ISN'T?

"One of the greatest lessons I learned from my dad was to make sure your children know that you love them."
—AL ROKER

My family comes from an interesting background—Italian Americans from New Jersey. We have a lot of stories, some told more than others. One that comes to mind is my dad's uncle who took a shower, snuck out the window, and never came back. My dad's cousin only found this out as my aunts and uncles (my father's siblings) sat around and shared stories from the good old times. Even closer to home, a family friend had a mental breakdown prior to the birth of his child, eventually leading to a divorce, custody battles, and permanent daddy issues for the child involved.

BEING A WIMP

There are times throughout your life when you may have, or have not, engaged in a fight, come across a volatile driver with road rage, exchanged harsh words in a grocery store, or been the subject of a rude quip from someone else. In the post-COVID-19 era, it seems like these encounters have increased and become more vitriolic. I generally felt on edge any time I went out in public. I had to deal with three kids, germs, crowds, and now unruly people who were mostly unhappy and unsure, and everything was subject to an invisible phobia, causing everyone to be extra touchy.

Unfortunately, for my wife and kids, I never stand down to unruly people. If someone passes a rude comment or an aside, I generally say something back. I try to be kind and honest, but I do not let some stranger go unchecked with rudeness, and I do not let someone else be rude to me or those around me. This might be a character flaw, because there is nothing to gain from having "words" with strangers; in fact, the opposite is true—there is only something to lose. Spending a night in jail or causing more stress for yourself and those around you is really the only thing that could happen.

Throughout my life, I've been lucky, knowing when to flee or when to fight. Sometime in college, I was driving home late at night through my neighborhood, and as I came around a back street, I noticed a car pull up behind me really close. I didn't think much of it until the car whipped around me fast, and as I looked inside, I saw that the car contained a group of young guys. It then proceeded to get in front of me and started braking. I slowed down and reasoned that there was no reason for me to stop the car—there were four guys in that one, and myself in my car.

I wasn't "He-Man."[32] So, I stopped, put the car in reverse, and backed up until I met a cross street where I could turn. The car proceeded to follow me. When it got right up behind me again, I floored it and headed for a busy street. They veered off. I'd avoided whatever encounter was waiting for me.

Ultimately, when it all comes down to it, responding to life's adversities with a sense of responsibility is like this: Know when to take a stand, know when to take a knee, and know when to flee. Choosing to do either of the latter does not make you less manly. In fact, it confirms that you are a wise and fearless leader who knows how to prioritize for the sake of those entrusted to your care. It means you are not one who makes decisions lightly or emotionally, and as a result, you'll be around for the next one. Your family can depend on you.

MY WAY OR THE HIGHWAY

Bro…don't make stubbornness your standard. Be stubborn sometimes, absolutely. Throughout your fatherhood, it will be imperative that you stand up for what you believe in. Absolutely and always stand for what you believe is best or right and protect the interests of you and yours. But be sure that if you are going to be stubborn, you know what is at stake. Whatever is at stake as the resultant effect of your stubbornness, be sure it's worth it.

---

[32] He-Man is an obscure 80's reference to *Masters of the Universe*, an animated series that aired from 1982–1988.

Standing up and being stubborn to the point that "...It's my way or the highway" are not synonymous, though we convince ourselves they are. Some of us like to wear our stubbornness with pride, and why not? For every time we were treated like less than a man or a person without a voice or whose opinion did not matter...or we were blamed for someone else's failures or mistakes...stubbornness is our defense against dismissal. Mental health professionals might call this weapon of mass destruction a defense mechanism.[33] Every war and game demands quality defense, right? Stubbornness is us taking a stand to protect our territory and win, right?

"Taking a stand" and "stubbornness" are two distinct concepts with different motivations and mental processes. One requires a more restricted mindset.[34] These cognitive limitations create actual barriers to seeing, seizing, or creating opportunities that could provide long-term benefits for oneself and others.

Consequently, when those affected realize that they have potentially missed out on beneficial opportunities due to these barriers, it can lead to feelings of alienation and isolation. The focus here is on understanding how rigid standards can impact relationships and recognizing the importance of considering others' perspectives and experiences.

"I can handle it! Chill and let me do this...look, it's my way or the highway!"

As fathers, it is our job to lead where necessary but also to defer and listen when applicable. We must find a balance

---

[33] "Defence Mechanism: What They Are And Why We Use Them," Psychologs, accessed October 16, 2025, https://www.psychologs.com/defence-mechanism-what-they-are-and-why-we-use-them/; "The Psychology Behind Stubbornness," Psychologs, January 18, 2024, https://www.psychologs.com/the-psychology-behind-stubbornness/.

[34] Arbinger Institute, "Mindset and the Basics of Arbinger's Work," Arbinger (blog), accessed October 16, 2025, https://arbinger.com/blog/mindset-and-the-basics-of-arbingers-work/#two-mindsets.

between softness and strength. You are not always right. You may have a strong opinion about something, and you can share that with your wife, but trying to convince your wife that your way is the only way to do something is not only incorrect but also rude and ignorant.

Mothers have an instinct to parent and to put the child first. Men generally have an instinct to put themselves first. I work every day to consider my family first—and it takes work—but now that I've done that for years, I've formed that habit. Stop, try to see everyone's opinions, and seek everyone's interest; this makes for greater communication but also a greater outcome. You will not feel good if you beat someone down so much that you won, rather than that you came to an amicable resolution—whatever that may be…and that is okay.

ACCOUNTABILITY

Dads should apologize. Saying you're sorry is not a sign of weakness. Apologizing doesn't mean you're suddenly less of a dad or somehow not strong. It is rather the opposite. Men who can apologize and embrace accountability probably get laid a lot more by their wives, girlfriends, or partners.[35] Seriously, it shows your kids that mistakes are okay, we are all human, and you, being the father, are not a brick wall—you have emotions, remorse, and do things wrong or incorrectly. Even so, when that happens, you have the strength to take accountability for it. When we think about leading by example, there is no better way to show kids respect than showing them humility, and acknowledging your faults is the only way to do that.

Along the lines of accountability, if you see something, do

---

[35] Maybe it really does all come down to sex.

something—you should just do it, not wait around for someone else to do it.

DADDY ISSUES

As I grew up, I experienced my father as being uninterested for the most part, except when he was so interested that it overpowered everything and everyone else. The big saying in our house was that dad really took an interest when you could have an intriguing conversation with him—so that would be around twelve-ish—unless it was something he was passionate about.

My father dropped me off at school once (this rarely happened). I was around ten years old. Another boy and I had gotten into a tussle, and he tripped me, and I lost my balance. That evening, after my father got home, he sat me down on the couch and asked repeatedly what had happened. I told him over and over again.

Apparently, he saw something different—in his mind, his child was the victim of a bully, and he could not take it. He was so worked up over this that by the end of the conversation, he was screaming that he would come with me to the principal's office, except that each word was punctuated by the pounding of his fist into the coffee table—so hard that his hands bled. I sat there. What else could I do but agree with him that someone maybe had picked on me? I would not think of the repercussions, and I cried.

It was better to experience his benevolence[36]—those led

---

36 "benevolence: disposition to do good." Merriam-Webster.com Dictionary, Merriam-Webster, https://www.merriam-webster.com/dictionary/benevolence. My father is a good man—he is family first, strong-willed, masculine, and stubborn. I say benevolence here because the overall disposition to do good was always there, throughout my childhood, though sometimes it was lost in an argument, or a strong opinion that ruled over everything else.

to better stories over the years, if they weren't slightly disturbing in their own right. My uncle loves to tell the time when my dad was describing his kids, who were seven and ten—we were actually twelve and fifteen, my sister was in high school… enough said.

But it wasn't all bad. In early high school, I was just starting to get really good at playing an instrument. Once a year, auditions were held for students to participate in an "Honor Band" where the best young musicians came together to showcase their talents. In my freshman year of high school, I was selected to be a part of the honor band. Prior to rehearsals starting, we all had to do a follow-up playing test to make sure that no one's time was wasted when we all got together to play in the larger band.

During the pre-rehearsal test, I could not get past this one musical part—I remember practicing, but probably not enough to make a difference, and I failed my test. I took the practice and the achievement for granted, and I was kicked out of the band for it. I was devastated. I remember disappointing my band teacher and how embarrassed I was.

More importantly, I remember talking to my dad. He said, "Lesson learned, now that this has happened to you, you know how it feels, and you do not have to let it happen again. Next time you pick up that instrument, it will be for a purpose." A different kid in the same situation might never have played an instrument again.

The next year, I chose to audition and was placed in the Honors Band. I was then selected for the All-State Band and even went on to play in a United States regional honor band. That moment did not define me, but it did shape me—lesson learned. And my dad helped me see that at a moment when I needed it most. My dad was probably the only one who could communicate that to me in that way to achieve a better result—and he was there for me.

The Boomer generation was different; talk about the stereotypical masculinity—strength = muscles; money = power. The man works, the woman raises kids. When I was starting my professional career, a much older colleague went out of his way to tell me that he did not want to sound misogynistic,[37] but there was something really "special" about a man coming home after work to a woman and the kids. Especially telling that he always had to preface this statement with the fact that he was not a chauvinist.

AUTHORITY

Authority figures for men really shape them. Whether your father, an uncle, or a teacher, male figures throughout your life shape your masculinity. This is an interesting dichotomy because at first, you probably try to defy all odds and expectations to avoid these connections, but ultimately, men become the thing they defy—it really is unavoidable. Young men want nothing to do with any authority figures. They are trying to figure out what authority means and do not want to be told what or how to do something. How many times have we rolled our eyes at our dads or some older man trying to explain his way to a logical outcome of what we think is complete foolishness?

I had (probably still have) some issues with authority, even though I was respectful and respected, especially throughout

---

[37] "misogynistic: feeling, showing, or characterized by hatred of or prejudice against women: of, relating to, or being a misogynist." https://www.merriam-webster.com/dictionary/misogynistic. In the professional world, it was always easy to fall into tropes with other men—talk about sports, watch a hot lady walk by, do things that measured the size of your dick rather than your skill. I'd like to think that has changed, or gotten better than twenty-five years ago when I was starting out, and I think for the most part it has.

my teenage years—I suppose all teenage boys do. I got a lot of traffic tickets—I was a teenage boy and the first to drive among my friends, so I had to take everyone home.

I remember taking everyone home one night and trying to get home before curfew—and in doing so, I was going fast down an open road. I was pulled over, and the officer was so pissed at me that I was pulled out of the car and thrown on the hood. I thought I was being respectful, but out of my mouth came a "Yes, Ma'am" as a response to a question. After hearing this, the officer lost it and yelled, "Excuse me!" He put his hand toward his firearm, and I did not say another word. Even at a moment where I should have shut up, I still had to rebel. I have no idea why, and in fact, I think it was subconscious, but it highlighted the very real fact—men have problems with authority. No one will tell us what to do—rather, we know what to do.

Why does any of this matter? Because we are preprogrammed to be fathers, whether we like it or not.[38] And if we do not like it, be prepared to make a concerted effort to overrule the stereotype. Speaking from personal experience, there have been times when I have lost my temper, reminding me of my father, or other times where I might have made a snide comment or a useless aside for no reason other than to make a point or to put someone down. That is not me; that is programming from what I saw others do. We can all think of those moments or actions and reactions, and we have to work to reprogram the response to what we want rather than what we have learned. This is where effort is required, and thoughtful recollections are necessary.

---

38 Many fathers I've talked to over the years agree with this assertion, and with the good, the bad, and the ugly. We are subjects of our environments. Only when we can step outside of the pattern and make a choice to be different or to do something differently than what we saw, heard, or had done to us are we actually different.

NO, YOU DID NOT MARRY YOUR MOTHER

How many times have we heard of the son who is too involved with their mother's life, or on the flip side, the mom who is too involved in their son's life? This topic is the subject matter of many books, articles, theories, psychiatry sessions, etc. Thanks to Sigmund Freud, the Oedipus Complex[39] is widely known that some boys have a strong attachment to their moms while having aggression toward their fathers. This theory is widely known but is mostly overblown and misunderstood. No one really understands that it happens in very early child development, predominantly around the ages of three to six years old, and it is very limited in time—until a young boy has a father figure to emulate in their continuous growth cycle.

Having had a son go through this "mommy" stage—it is just that—my concern is more for those boys who will not move out of the basement or who insist that their mother has to do their laundry for them, cook for them, or clean for them. My wife calls these guys "Mammones"—translated to mamma's boy—and I trust her judgment on this.

A troubling statistic came out that sixty percent of young men (ages eighteen to twenty-four)[40] still live with their parents—this is higher than for young women. So, it is not just that young people live at home—yes, they do, but more men do than women. Again, men have got to get out of the basement. And more importantly, they have to take responsibility

---

[39] Forgive me, I apologize if you have no idea what I am talking about. Sigmund Freud, one of the most famous psycho analysts of all time, came up with the theory that boys experience sexual desires toward their mothers while simultaneously experiencing rivalry toward their fathers—the Oedipus Complex, and is widely studied.

[40] Society has pushed this infantilization of men so much that men are having a hard time transitioning into adulthood because they are not experiencing those things that make them adults. The rise of over-protective parenting, coupled with the rising costs of living and societal shift, has made men less independent and more codependent.

for themselves for the benefit of those around them, not for the sake of it. If you are a dad who expects your wife to take care of all the house things because you work, you need to get over yourself and contribute to the home in ways other than just monetarily.

If you do not know how to do laundry, learn. If you do not know how to cook, practice. There is no excuse for not contributing if you do not, and saying that you contribute in other ways is just an excuse that you tell yourself to get out of doing chores—doing the shit that you do not want to do.

When it comes to my kids, sometimes, I feel like I had just enough of a lack of influence in my childhood that I created my own destiny. I always try to acknowledge when I cross a proverbial line—my wife understands and appreciates it. We all can improve, and if there are serious gaps in why or how you do something, you know you can do better—the first step is to try and do it better. Psychiatry is great, sure, but it all starts with you—no one is to blame for how you act or react. All you can do is try to be the best person you can be, and it will bring out the best in those around you, especially your kids.

MANtra

I am my own man.

Actionable Items:

- *I am my own man* because I am not my father.
    - We cannot deny who our spheres of influence are; it is better to acknowledge them, accept the good, and remove the bad. Connect with a father figure in your life and have a conversation with them.

- *I am my own man* because I am not defined by others.
    - Limiting our sphere of influence to one person is unrealistic. We are all influenced by others, and during impressionable years, there may be other people who have had a positive or negative influence—coaches, teachers, aunts, and uncles. Remember, you are who you are because of you, not them.

- *I am my own man* because I choose to be.
    - Do not let that sphere of influence consume you—if you are reading this book and saying it is all someone else's fault, you are missing the point. We choose our own path. Reflect on three important decisions in your life that you made by yourself. What happened is irrelevant—your choice to do it is what matters.

CHAPTER 7

PHYSICAL WELL-BEING

"Having children is like living in a frat house. Nobody sleeps, everything's broken, and there's a lot of throwing up."
—RAY ROMANO

Physical insecurity[41] leads to a lack of confidence that leads to a decrease in mental health. This is the reality of the world that we live in. Simply put, insecurity = depression. Study after study has shown a direct and causal link between insecurity and a decline in mental health, reflected in low self-esteem,

---

41 "insecurity: the quality or state of being insecure, such as a state or feeling of anxiety, fear, or self-doubt." Merriam-Webster.com Dictionary, Merriam-Webster, https://www.merriam-webster.com/dictionary/insecurity. I spent a lifetime feeling insecure, I look in the mirror to this day and still feel things I felt when I was thirteen years old. Some things are just a part of you—what I do now is accept the things I can control and let go of those I cannot.

depression, eating disorders, and overall negative emotions. This is at the core of why I wrote this book—in a world where we are told that our dadbods are sexy, that a little extra flab around the mid-section is kind of "hot," we feel insecure and awkward by the reality that those things exist.

BODY ISSUES

How in one breath can someone say we are one thing when, in reality, we feel different? Consider this carefully: all those things you did to get to where you are today shaped who you are—they do not define you.

I remember walking the High Line in New York City several years ago. It's a beautiful outdoor park along Hell's Kitchen in NYC, and it butts up right against The Standard Hotel.[42] The hotel is situated in such a way that it is on the walking trail, and the trail goes right under the hotel. On a clear summer day, you can see into the hotel windows, and on this particular day, lo and behold, I look up to see a naked man standing in the window. There was some distance between us, but I could clearly make out that this was indeed a nude man—and so could my wife and probably my daughter. Without making a huge deal of it, my wife and I acknowledged what we were seeing and enjoyed a shared chuckle between us. But for that guy standing proudly above the High-Line in his birthday suit—for all onlookers to see—I salute you. Your body confidence is epic.

I do not have that. For most of my life, I lived around people

---

[42] The Standard Hotel in NYC is a great spot to stay for the weekend if you're looking to reconnect with your wife. https://www.standardhotels.com/new-york/properties/high-line. I've walked The High Line many times with and without kids: https://www.thehighline.org/. If you are ever in the NYC area, it is worth checking out.

who had an overt sense of modesty. Everything was covered up, and no one showed "extra" skin. My wife is the opposite; growing up as a dancer, she is very comfortable in her own skin—she says it's because she grew up in front of a dance mirror.

Today, my body confidence is better, but only because I got to a place of mental, emotional, and physical security where I did not feel ashamed of my body. Many people go through life with confidence issues—mainly physical insecurity about how they look. We do have to find acceptance of who we are physically to ensure that the lack of physical security does not cause undue stress or anxiety in our daily lives. If we are not secure, we are not confident, and therefore not our best selves.

STRESSORS

I'm an attorney—arguably one of the most stressful[43] jobs in the US, if you let it be. In fact, one of the jobs I had was so stressful that I literally had to quit after three months. Stress might look different for everyone, but the health consequences are the same.

My blood pressure skyrocketed; I was traveling every weekend and living in a new city where I knew no one. I made good money, so I wanted to stick it out and had already sacrificed[44] a lot to make it happen in the first place. But I will never forget the time when I tried to give blood at the local blood drive (work-sponsored), and the technician told me I could not donate blood, but instead, I should go to the hospital.

---

43 "stress: a physical, chemical, or emotional factor that causes bodily or mental tension and may be a factor in disease causation." Merriam-Webster.com Dictionary, Merriam-Webster, https://www.merriam-webster.com/dictionary/stress. Are you in need of a break to level off, or are you feeling good?

44 "sacrifice: destruction or surrender of something for the sake of something else." https://www.merriam-webster.com/dictionary/sacrifice. Being a parent requires sacrifice, and being a good dad means choosing to go further. Why? Because moms are expected to be "good," dads are expected to just show up.

Currently, I have a colleague in a similar position—we rely on this person for many important tasks throughout our work. They shared with me that their blood pressure was through the roof, and they are taking some time to level off. There has to be a better way than doing something that literally might kill you one day.

There are moments in our lives where we reach special and unique fulcrum points that we did not think possible. Things can boil over sometimes—whether it is a co-worker getting under your skin, a job you hate, a sudden change in circumstance, a lay-off, a fight with your spouse, or financial stressors. These things have a direct and real impact on your physical well-being.

Hypertension is the leading cause of death in the United States. Americans (men especially) are terrible at moderation and acknowledging that anything is wrong. We will work through it, put our heads down, and keep going before we admit something is wrong. I respect that to a degree, but without addressing the root causes of any of these issues, they will build, grow, and come out sideways.

Being a father with a high-stress job is especially difficult. There may be any given day that you may come home to a mess of a house, a kid screaming, a random song playing, dogs barking, whatever it might be—as a father, it is always in addition to, not in lieu of. You need to be able to compartmentalize what happened at work because something will more than likely happen at home. Sure, there are those good days when it may be extra quiet, but those are few and far between; the reality is that kids are loud, messy, and unapologetic. Being a good father is knowing that is the case and being okay with that. Because if you are not, it will be one more added stressor to an already stressful life.

Back to physical well-being… Remember all that analysis on the dadbod and how it was cool to have some tummy fat or some extra love handles? Those same love handles and extra weight add pressure to your heart and arteries. That dadbod of yours could be an extenuating factor for health and wellness that can eventually cause a real and substantive need for corrective action. In my case, I gained forty-five pounds over the course of ten years. With the weight gain came an emotional lack of self-confidence, but physically, higher blood pressure, getting winded going up the stairs, and general fatigue.

I made a conscious choice to tackle my dadbod at a time when I needed it most. My kids wanted someone to keep up, and I knew they needed someone for as long as possible.

A family friend of ours died suddenly. He was forty-two years old. He had a stroke in the early morning hours; the doctors said it may have been a past head trauma causing a tube in his brain to disconnect. He got out of bed one morning, fell over, and eventually died. He left behind two young boys. I tell you this because it reminded me that time is precious—and the only way to make the most of that time is to ensure that you prioritize your physical health. So as "sexy" as the dadbod is, if you feel that it has made your physical well-being suffer, you need to make adjustments. Any adjustment made is not only for you, but for your kids also, to be present in their lives as long as you possibly can.

MANtra

Live every day like you mean it.

Actionable Items:

- *Live every day like you mean it* so your kids know they are loved.
  - One important thing in our household is never to go to bed angry, and that includes the kids as well, them being mad at us or each other. Many times throughout my life, I've often wondered if I should say something or do something differently. We live by this in our household so that nothing is left unsaid that may have real and deleterious effects on relationships down the road. Kids recover fast and may or may not remember what they did or said twenty minutes ago—we do. Be sure to say what is on your mind when it happens—do not hold it in.

- *Live every day like you mean it* so you feel alive.
  - All of us have gone through the ropes at some point. Looking back, those are the moments that have the least impact because they did not create core memories—in reality, there was nothing worth remembering. Create a core memory by stepping outside of the box to do something new and/or different from what you are used to. Go bowling on a weekday, take that trip you've been

saving up for—do something that creates real and core memories for you and your family.

- *Live every day like you mean it* so you don't regret it.
    - All of us have regrets, and many of us live with a should've, could've, would've mentality. Think of a scenario where you should have done something differently. Whatever it is, take that moment back and say it, do it, live it. It is never too late.

CHAPTER 8

BE MORE THAN JUST A MIDDLE-AGE TROPE

"Today is the oldest you've ever been, and the youngest you'll ever be again."
—ELEANOR ROOSEVELT

Several phases throughout your life are of utmost importance. I recently read that aging happens in spurts rather than systemically throughout your life. At a few fulcrum points, one may experience a quick and sudden change in health that comes on statistically at age forty-four and age sixty.

For men, these years are also pivotal because they are gateways to new phases of their lives. By forty, you are supposed to have your shit figured out—for men, you are supposed to have a job, maybe even a successful career, a loving wife, and perhaps a kid or two or three. And, stereotypically, you are also predisposed to have a midlife crisis and are supposed to be tired of all that boring comfort and go out and buy a convertible, get ripped, and have an affair.

How many times have we seen or heard of the story: boy meets girl, gets married, has kids, gets divorced, and over and over again, the pattern goes. It is all too common in this day and age, so much so that half of all marriages end in divorce, and of those marriages, the number one reason they ended was lack of commitment. Even further, women overwhelmingly initiated the divorce process. Are we sensing a pattern here? Women, who are fed up with deadbeat dads, divorce them—try to convince me the dadbod is sexy.

Dads, of course, have their part in this too. I would be surprised to hear that "99% Mom" did not divorce her husband by now—the discontent was palpable. "Checkmark-Man" more than likely had an affair by now—he had to do something with his time. But the harsh reality is that when "99% Mom" and "Checkmark-Man" are married for a few years, it seems pretty obvious why the marriage did not work out. The parents could not bring themselves to make a difference to satisfy their own and each other's needs. The only problem is that the kids are the ones who suffer.

Being a dad is only one piece of the puzzle, and the title of this book is not lost on me—but the dad makes up one part of a family. The mom is as integral, or more integral, to a modern-day household and any children as a subset of that core relationship. Pro-dad groups will scorn me for this opinion, but dads also have to know their place. Statistically, if a couple splits up with kids, chances are that the wife will receive full custody. Before you do anything that pulls you away from your fatherly and familial duties, please consider the real facts that society is already against you if you mess up. As dads, we have the awesome responsibility to take care of our families, but we are also the first in line to lose them if we fail them. It is a fickle reality that we live in. As men, we can take it and we can step up to the challenge.

As we all enter into the post-honeymoon phase of marriage and accept the lull and comfort of the dadbod, it is especially important to avoid becoming another stereotype. Around 20 percent of men cheat on their wives—and yes, that number is higher than married women experiencing infidelity. If that is or was you, I sincerely hope you figured out a way to lead with character throughout the process—whatever that is. As we work through your manhood awareness and discover positive changes in you, others will notice. Women will notice. This is not a book on how to get laid by someone other than your wife—this book is about having great sex with your wife. It's not just about losing the dadbod (if that is what you want to do). It's about gaining incredible confidence, embracing your masculinity, and genuinely starting to show up for and care about your kids so you don't end up another middle-aged statistic. There is no easier way to undermine everything you do than to take all of it for granted. But how do we get there? Let's start with some basics…

HEALTH AND WELLNESS

First off, I am not a fitness guru. There have been many years in my life that I did not have a gym membership, or even anything fitness-related in the same presence as myself. I tell you this because I know the type of dude we all think of when we think of health and wellness. The typical gym rat who has a six-pack, wears tank tops and shorts any chance they get, and always has a backward hat on. The point of this book is not to become that person; let's be clear about that. Mental and physical health are as important as each other because you really cannot have one without the other.

RELATIONSHIPS

To be healthy, we must focus on why we may be unhealthy. These come in all forms; they can be our relationship with food, our family, our kids, or even our relationship with our colleagues. Relationships are a major driver in overall mental and physical health. A stressful day at work means you probably are craving something sweet or comfortable to make you feel better. Fast forward several years in a stressful job, how many extra calories did you take in, not because you wanted to, but because you needed something to take the edge off of your day?

I used work as an example, but extrapolate the idea to any relationship that exists in your circle: family, kids, and friends. The less stressful your relationships are, the more you can focus on driving results to your benefit, which is the key to success in finding a positive health and wellness relationship between yourself and food.

MAKE A PLAN

What is just as important is having a plan to make small strides in your desired direction. Health and wellness come in many forms. I say this because many times throughout my life, I have seen scenarios where I thought one thing existed one way, but the reality was far different from what I imagined.

One time, we hired piano movers to move our piano, and the team that showed up was an oddball mix of young men, except for a very small older gentleman. I had assumed that the older gentleman was the boss and would boss around the younger guys, but the opposite happened. Coming in almost a full foot shorter than everyone else, at five feet nothing, at some point, he single-handedly had an upright piano on his back and proceeded to carry it down a flight of stairs. The other men were just a guide for this master of strength to do a mini masterclass in piano moving.

As we embark on a health and wellness journey, remember the five-foot-tall piano-mover-man. Health comes in all shapes and sizes, and effects happen in all kinds of different ways. You may never have a six-pack, and that is okay. If your BMI is at a healthy place and you feel stronger, then it doesn't matter.

Everything is a journey, and there is no right or wrong way to go about this process. We choose to make adjustments because we know those adjustments are worth it in the end to achieve a more fulfilled existence, whatever form that may take. Remind yourself often that you are in control of what you do and how you do it.

MANtra

I will take care of myself, but not at the expense of my family.

Actionable Items:

- *I will take care of myself, but not at the expense of my family,* to ensure I am happy.
  - Sometimes, we have to do a better job of taking time out for ourselves—and that is a must in fatherhood. Creating opportunities for "me" time is crucial, but remember, we all have to make sacrifices. If you are spending all of your free time at the gym, spa, or a bar hanging out with your guy friends, you are missing out on the most important part of your child's life. Balance to happiness is key, and finding the right opportunities is a must. Do not sacrifice time with your family to make time for yourself—there are other, better ways to do it. Do the small tasks that add up. These include, but are not limited to, washing the dishes or loading/unloading the dishwasher, taking out the trash, and folding the laundry. Each of these small tasks must be done and are never fun, but should be shared amongst everyone in the family. Make sure you do your part.

- *I will take care of myself, but not at the expense of my family,* because I have control over my body.
  - This is something that took me a long time to realize—I have control over my body in as much detail as I see fit.

I control what goes into my body, what happens to my body, what I put on my body, and the list goes on, and this is something that we often take for granted. Before you eat anything, ask yourself if you want it or need it. Do this for everything that goes into your body for the next seven days.

- *I will take care of myself, but not at the expense of my family,* because I have control over my mind.
  - Just as you control the physical, you also control the mental part of yourself. Many of us have unruly thoughts, ideas, and instincts. This is common and does not mean anything other than being human. However, we can program our minds to think happy thoughts. Start this process by being cognizant of mental awareness enough to stop yourself from derailing into negative thoughts. Next time you find your mind wandering, try to center yourself on a happy moment.

CHAPTER 9

MEN'S HEALTH

"Physical fitness is not only one of the most important keys to a healthy body, it is the basis of dynamic and creative intellectual activity."
—JOHN F. KENNEDY

When I used to work out, prior to having kids, I had a singular focus—to look good. I was not concerned about my overall health, and as a result, I never really took my workouts seriously. If your focus were only on the surface, it would be impossible to find a drive or dedication to achieve a positive outcome. At the end of the day, the entire experience was a wash, accompanied by a meaningless head shrug.

EXERCISE

Later in life, you might find that approaching exercise comes with a renewed sense of caution and responsibility. For the same reason why those people who go to college later in life get better grades or seek out more fruitful opportunities, working out post-forty has more meaning.

Your approach to it matters more. Those older people in college are not any smarter than their younger counterparts; they only have life experience telling them that going to college at forty matters more now than it did before—there is more to gain, but also more to lose. The same goes for gym workouts.

You have to consider which exercises matter most—those that target the right areas without aggravating past injuries or creating new ones. Moderation and temperance matter more because recovery times might take longer than they used to, and certain muscle groups might move slower than they used to.

The best way to ensure a smooth transition back to exercise and away from the dadbod is to focus on the essential body weight exercises. Most importantly, the push-up and the pull-up.

PUSH-UP

The push-up is one of the oldest and most consistent exercises ever. In ancient India, soldiers lined up and pushed off the ground for training. Also, Constantine, the most prolific Roman Emperor, did push-ups daily and required Roman soldiers to follow suit. The push-up requires total body engagement while focusing on the manliest part of the body—your chest and upper arms. While engaging the pectoral, deltoid, triceps, biceps, coracobrachialis, and serratus anterior muscles, the push-up has no equal when it comes to male physique. Push-ups are even expected to boost testosterone levels because of the way they engage in aerobic and resistance training for the upper body, specifically.

Why am I dedicating a whole section of this book to basic, silly exercises like push-ups and pull-ups? Because at a time when I hit rock bottom, my only goal was to do a singular perfect push-up. One push-up? Who cares? No big deal. Most men cannot do a proper push-up. I could not for many years. The extra weight caused my body to curve while doing the exercise; my arms were not strong enough to support that extra girth, and my knees wanted to touch the ground just to take the pressure off. Yes, it is one push-up, but if they are not correct, there is a limited possibility for achievement and advancement in your physical and mental health.

The proper push-up begins with you lying horizontally on the floor face down with your arms side to side.[45] Keep your legs firm and focus the movement on your arms, but the muscles used in your chest area will enhance the overall push-up and ensure you are doing it correctly. Try to keep your body as stiff as a board throughout this process.

Now that we've covered those basics, the push-up for me was the first time I realized that I had the dadbod and also that I needed to lose the dadbod. Sometime around 2020, I was in the middle of quarantine and badly needed to work out. I think it came from a sense that everything was upside down, and maybe there was one thing I could control—or maybe I was looking for one outlet where I knew I could release some endorphins—who knows? Not being able to actually go to a

---

45 I really feel like I do not have to explain this to you—you know what a push-up is, but sometimes it is good to hear the basics again, even just to confirm that you are doing it correctly.

gym, I started looking for guides. I found a simple app that had bodyweight workouts, and the main focus was the push-up.

Throughout this time, my kids were young enough that they wanted to do it with me. My kids would either jump on my back, line up next to me, or they'd crawl underneath me, and they loved to almost be squished until I could lift off the ground (this was great motivation for proper form, and having an extra thirty pounds on your back while you try to push up does not make it easier).

PULL-UP

The pull-up, like the push-up, is a basic body-weight exercise. It too has a deep past in old-world ideals combined with military and calisthenic origins. But unlike the push-up, it is far more difficult to achieve a perfect pull-up. It starts standing under a bar that is just barely taller than your extended arm length above your head, grabbing that bar and pulling yourself up so that your chin goes over the bar, and then dropping slowly back down.

The perfect pull-up is almost impossible without achieving a certain level of fitness. Every time I think of a pull-up, for whatever reason, I go back to being a kid again, and those adolescent years when we were required to do pull-ups as a mark of physical fitness.

I remember when I was about eleven or so, I started to gain that extra pre-pubescent weight, and it was time for the fitness test. Sadly, I could not do a pull-up. The sheer embarrassment racked my young soul—and scarred me for life. I could barely face my friends, was reminded daily of my excess weight, and I spiraled into an overall dislike of fitness after that. I wasn't picked on about it, and there were a handful of other boys who were in the same position as me; it was not that big of a deal at the end of the day. What happened to me, though, was the stark realization that I was weak—and I hated that feeling. My embarrassment was self-inflicted but stayed with me for most of my life.

Around age twenty-five, I wanted to get back into fitness. I found a box and subscribed to the latest health trend, which was an exercise regimen to push yourself because you can, not because you should. It encouraged you to push your body to its limits, so it was entirely acceptable for an average Joe like me to start Olympic weightlifting or dive into a freezing pool.

For those of you who know what I am talking about, it was a way of life. Just not my way of life. As I continued with this regimen for months, pull-ups became an often-occurring activity. By the time I stopped, I could do many pull-ups in a row. They probably were not perfect, but I felt like I had gained a certain amount of physical strength, and I was happy. When I gained my dadbod, I lost that success—and again, that gnawing feeling came back. I was eleven years old again, weak and out of control.

It took two years from start to finish to be able to do a perfect pull-up again. But with that perfect pull-up also came a renewed sense of control, strength, and confidence. See, it was never about the pull-up itself, it was about what doing it or not being able to do it meant to my mental and emotional state.

Please do not go to the gym and try to lift the most weights you have ever lifted, or try to do as many exercises as you possibly can, just to prove you can still do it. This is a sure way to get injured and lose motivation to ever go again. If you push yourself hard out of the gate, you will fatigue—your body will not be as motivated to go back to the gym, and you will see minimal gains—this is a guarantee. Exercise gains, like anything else in life, require patience and temperance. Start slow, take your time, and please be patient with yourself.

FATHERHOOD = MASCULINITY

In those moments, all of us were aligned to make Daddy healthy. To my kids, it was a game, but they saw me push myself (literally), follow the rules, and work toward something. Remember this in anything you do from this point forward—little eyes are watching you. That is not meant to add pressure to the situation because whether you do it or not, they would still love you. But how and why you do it matters now—ten, fifteen, twenty years ago, it may not have mattered in the same way.

That is why fatherhood matters most and approaching something that you may have previously taken for granted matters more now than it used to.

MANtra

I have control over my health and wellness.

Actionable Items:

- *I have control over my health and wellness,* so I will work toward a specific goal when it comes to my physical body.
  - Please think long and hard about a single physical fitness goal that has been gnawing at you. For example, running around a track in a certain amount of time, completing one unassisted pull-up, doing a set of twenty-five push-ups continually, and the like. Start it and track your success.

- *I have control over my health and wellness,* so I will not eat overly processed foods.
  - Ask your wife if she has a label maker. If so, go through and put labels of your kids' names or your wife's name on anything that you snack on to fill a void, rather than for any nutritional value. This simple step makes your mind acknowledge that someone else will eat that, and by labeling it, you are making yourself go over another hurdle to eat it—you are taking it away from someone else.

- *I have control over my health and wellness,* so I can live up to my full potential.

- Healthy food makes healthy bodies—the only way to retain a healthy mindset is to ensure that you eat healthy food.

CHAPTER 10

THE DADBOD DIET

"The only time to eat diet food is while you're waiting for the steak to cook."
—JULIA CHILD

Throughout my adult life, I have tried many different diets, and we all know there are a thousand different ways to approach food. One of the most important things I realized early on is that I have a pretty healthy relationship with food in general, and for those of you who do not, this part of the process is a much larger challenge. It is not insurmountable, but it is necessary to tackle the root cause of how you see food. Most importantly, we must all live by the very familiar adage: we eat to live, not live to eat. No requirement in life demands that you eat anything except food for your body and brain to function.

Nothing requires that you have to try the latest craze dessert or a new and interesting pastry invention that has blown up Instagram. We choose to eat those things because they make us happy and cool and elevate our status. We do not have to eat those things. Moderation is key to everything, so a pastry treat is absolutely a healthy part of any meal plan. However, when that is all we eat, we have a problem.

DIET

You are what you eat. I'm sure we all have heard that saying in some way, shape, or form. Literally speaking, I guess the saying is true, but I never actually believed it until I tried a few things out and lived up to another trope I commonly heard—any weight loss plan is 90 percent diet.

As a working dad, I love processed[46] food, specifically breakfast foods. I am not ashamed to admit it—the glorious idea of a warm Pop-Tart or a bowl of Cheerios, or better yet, Frosted Flakes, was one of the most magical things I looked forward to at any time.

Over the years, I cannot possibly imagine how many bowls of cereal I have consumed—the poundage on that alone is mind-boggling. Especially if you think about starting the count from when I was a kid, I could probably fill a dump truck full of Cheerios. I am not ashamed of it—but I am not proud of it either. It is just a by-product of the circumstances that befall all of us dads. We eat the food around us and what others around us eat. Do you think it is a coincidence that desserts is the word "stressed" spelled backward?

---

[46] "processed: having been subjected to a special process or treatment (as in the course of manufacture)." Merriam-Webster.com Dictionary, Merriam-Webster, https://www.merriam-webster.com/dictionary/processed. Processed food is just that—processed. It is fake, unnatural, and manufactured. It took me a long time to realize this, but only after I really started to think about my health and what I put into my body did this start to matter.

Furthermore, how many times was there an extra crust, extra dripping on a spoon, half a bowl of mac and cheese just lying around? And if you are like me, often doing the dishes, instead of throwing scraps away in the compost bin, I would eat them. Dads are constantly surrounded by unhealthy food, be prepared for this. This is another reason your dadbod has gone unchecked because even if you are watching what you eat, you are the gatekeeper for the rest of the family—and items undoubtedly make their way in.

Before we dive deeper into a structured meal plan, lose the habit of snacking on processed foods, and remember that you are not the garbage bin for your family. It is okay to leave certain foods where they are and to throw away other food—you do not have to eat all of it—and you do not have to feel bad that you are throwing it away.

Yes, what about the kids in Africa? Any meaningful contribution is far better off by a donation to UNICEF[47] rather than feeling guilty after throwing scraps away. You can be like my wife, who is a religious composter—heck, you can even leave out food for stray animals; just please do not feel guilty about the scraps—let them go.

Throughout my diet journey, I never gave up a few essential items that were imperative in how I wanted to live my life. I always put milk in my coffee, I love the occasional glass of red wine, and I still eat chocolate peanut butter cups. You have to choose your battles. If I forced myself to cut out everything I loved, I would not be where I am today.

When I first approached dieting again post fatherhood and full dadbod, I really wanted to take the pressure off of myself.

---

[47] Here is a link to UNICEF if you ever feel bad about throwing some food away: https://www.unicef.org/.

I did this by not being the garbage disposal—one easy fix was to not eat anyone's leftovers. Period.

Another quick fix was only to eat when I was hungry, not at a specific time, but rather when I was moved or motivated to eat. These simple adjustments make for quick and easy gains that I saw almost immediately. First, I did not take in any extra calories, and second, I automatically burned any additional water weight, and bloating almost immediately.

Yes, this happens with any diet, but for me at that point in my life, instant gratification was the fuel that pushed me harder. And these two simple adjustments forced me to continue to search for meaningful diets. At one point, I only ate chicken, rice, and broccoli. Sometime around 2005, this was the latest diet craze—lean protein and ultra-rich nutrients, vegetables, and throw in some rice with that.

It did nothing. The lean protein was just that—lean. The vegetables were great for keeping me regular, and the rice was a carbohydrate bomb that added extra bloating and prevented my body from actually burning any fat. It burned the rice instead, and the lean protein did not build muscle; it barely maintained it.

I knew what not to do, but I was so jaded by other things that I had tried already. I had no interest in dieting or following a meal plan, because nothing sounded right or interesting enough to follow. This time, I approached my nutrition very pragmatically. I was going to eat healthy, fresh foods with a rich protein diet and green vegetables, and I wanted to focus on the protein part.

I soon discovered that lots of things that I really enjoy eating have high levels of protein, specifically cheeses, avocados, and eggs. I then focused on ultra-high meat proteins like beef and salmon, and ultra-high fat proteins like bacon and sausage.

Focusing on these subsets of food groups and understanding the reasons for them was crucial in my nutritional journey. I knew I had to eliminate carbs. I also knew that if I wanted my body to burn fat, I needed to give it fat instead of carbs to do so, and I needed ultra-rich protein to retain muscle mass, plus build muscle. I never wanted to be or look skinny—looking frail or weak is not attractive to anyone, right? So, maintaining high levels of fat and protein were the two driving factors of my diet.

SOUNDS LIKE YOU ARE EATING KETO...

It took me about a year to admit I was "eating Keto." Again, labeling my diet for me was a non-starter. I had no interest in following a fad—fads do not work. The right mindset works; goals work; plans work. To this day, I still refuse to read any literature on Keto—I do not care. Sure, I understand its concept, and I understand how and why it works. One part of my diet that I would say was different from traditional Keto is that I eat no nuts, chia seeds, flax seeds, etc.

I do not like the taste of those things, and I remember reading an article several years ago about how chia seeds stick to your colon, so I maintained my distance from them. I have a semi-nut allergy to pecans, walnuts and cashews, which keeps me away from nuts, except for peanut butter. Admittedly, I still eat store-bought (natural) creamy peanut butter from one of the main distributors known—true peanut butter connoisseurs know the brand I am referring to—in moderation, of course.

Another thing I had to do was set aside all of the preconceived notions of cholesterol, fat, etc., behind me. I was fully aware that my diet at times was on the verge of too much processed meat, and that could have other side effects to worry about, like too much sodium or excess fat. However, the gains of losing poundage are so far greater than a slight rise in sodium or cholesterol that I was willing to take the risk at the start, just to test my instincts. Over eighteen months, I lost sixty-seven pounds. My goal was twenty.

I weighed in at two hundred and twenty-five pounds with full dadbod, and at the end of my weight loss journey, I weighed in at one hundred and fifty-eight. I was transformed—I had lost the weight of a kid—and the dadbod was officially gone. After the MANtra section, I included a basic two-week meal plan. Take it or leave it—it's up to you.

MEAL PLAN

It took me a long time to actually think about the food I eat and the quantities of food I consume. The only way I was successful in my diet was by tracking my food religiously using a food app[48] and weighing my food meticulously. Please invest in a food scale,[49] a good blender, and cooking utensils like an egg pan, frying pan, spatulas, and whisks.[50] You will be happy that you did.

There are a few key points to remember as you follow this meal plan. It is, in fact, a plan and aptly named as such. Think of it as a plan of action that requires preparation, dedication, and execution. Many things listed here are cooked, readily packaged and edible, or pre-portioned already. For example, sausage, chicken wings, and various types of chicken meatballs and chicken sausages come fully cooked and refrigerated, so

---

48   I used Cronometer.com: https://cronometer.com/.

49   Here's a good resource for everything you need to get started: https://dadbodshop.com/.

50   Here's a good resource for everything you need to get started: https://getpastrytools.com/.

you just need to heat them. Additionally, vegetables can come frozen, pre-packaged, cooked, or uncooked.

Choose food items that you know will not be cumbersome in the kitchen. Hamburger patties come pre-portioned, and the same goes for chicken breast, fresh filets, etc. They generally are around four to six ounces each. I never gave up alcohol, but I limited my intake to weekends and only to one or two glasses of red wine. Mixed drinks and hard alcohol do not go well on a high-protein, low-carb diet. Another thing I always did was to ensure that my grams of protein matched my weight. If you are a 200-lb guy, that's a lot of protein, but in order for this diet to work, it is imperative that you take in a lot of protein and hardly any carbs.

So, always make sure your carbohydrate intake (in grams) is a third of the protein. For example, if you weigh 150 lbs., you need at least 150 grams of protein and a max 50 grams of carbs. Additionally, you have to drink a lot of water, shoot for at least 80–100 ounces a day, more so if you weigh considerably higher than 250 lbs.

If you're not sure how to start, I've added a two-week meal plan in the appendix to help you get going.

ALCOHOL

The only alcohol I consumed (and still consume) on this diet is red wine. It is the most protein-friendly, and if you want real results, only one or two glasses per weekend, no more than six ounces per pour.

CHEAT DAYS

I left the weekends out because with kids, life gets in the way. Please see these days as time with your friends and family, days when the diet is not the most important thing, but rather the quality time that it is. If you cheat a little bit, it will not make you a failure—go easy on yourself and the process, and allow for a cheat day. For myself, weekends were the obvious time to let go a little bit.

VITAMINS

Many health food stores have starter packs or kits for men to get their required vitamins and nutrients. If you are one of those guys who cannot eat a vegetable, consider taking a multivitamin, and to jump-start working out, you can also take a daily testosterone boost. Please follow all necessary guidelines for these products. I am no expert.

MANtra

I will set aside preconceived notions about dieting.

Actionable Items:

- *I will set aside preconceived notions about dieting* and try something new.
  - The first step of doing something, anything, is to do it. Even if you have no desire to start a meal plan or a diet, you can make simple adjustments to try something new, or at least different from what you have been doing over the last five to fifteen years. It's easy to get discouraged while dieting—trying something (anything) new is a good way to jumpstart your new mentality for change and a way to achieve small gains fast. Stick to something—you will be grateful you did.

- *I will set aside preconceived notions about dieting* for the benefit of myself and others around me.
  - If you are overweight in the slightest, you have to consider the real and serious consequences that even a small amount of extra weight can have on your body. In addition to extra poundage requiring your heart to work harder to pump blood through you, your knees have to hold up a heavier amount, and your arteries have to squeeze blood through smaller veins. We all know this, but sometimes we forget that the body is the largest

butterfly effect we have in the world—a small change makes a huge difference in just about everything. Everything is reversible.

- *I will set aside preconceived notions about dieting* and commit to a plan for at least twenty-eight days.
  - I am asking for less than a month to jumpstart your journey—in the bigger picture of fatherhood, that is a blip on the radar. Commit to something long enough to start forming habits around it, and you will see the results you crave.

LAST THOUGHT

"A calm mind brings inner strength and self-confidence, so that's very important for good health."
—DALAI LAMA

Take anything you like from this book and leave the rest behind. I am not going to force my journey on anyone. The point I tried to make throughout this book is that we are all on our own journey, but we do not accept the fact that we are allowed to be forced into a stereotype just because we have nothing better to do with our lives. Everything you do as a person and as a man should be a choice that you make, and every choice you make should have the consequence and outcome that you desire. If that is not the case, you have the ability to change it, and hopefully, I gave you some tools and ideas to start your reverse dadbod journey—if and when you are ready to do so.

Throughout my personal journey, I grappled with the very real idea that having strong emotions that you are boring, comfortable, or weak comes from a long and drawn-out stigma that suggests that family men are not strong men. This cannot be further from the truth. Strength comes in many forms—and yes, it is obviously displayed in physical strength. But most importantly, it is displayed in your strength of character, how you treat others, and your everyday thinking. When the kids are caught in a detrimental circle, it requires you and/or your wife to accept that the moment is just a moment, and it will pass. Your dadbod is no different—it is a moment in a lifetime of being a father, and it can and will change. The strength of the modern dad is not defined by singularity, but rather the plurality of the fatherhood journey, and a balance of strength and softness is key to being a good father. And more importantly, a good man.

Sharing, to me, is what drives emotional and social connections and is what brings people together. Even down to the granular action of liking a post or sharing a pic on social media, we are doing something that is absolutely necessary for our personal acknowledgement and growth, and also our external demand to appease ourselves and others. How and what you share is what matters most—and to a modern-day dad, sharing is hard. Nothing is more important to your kids than the last thing that just happened. They do not care about your fight at work, your personal best, or how much money is in the bank account. They are singularly focused on the issue in front of them—maybe you can be too. I enjoyed sharing my story with you—I hope it helps you be the best man you can be.

MANtras

Everything is reversible.

I will be productive and useful.

Be the man you aspire to be today.

I respect myself.

Adolescence + Masculinity = Fatherhood.

I am my own man.

Live every day like you mean it.

I will take care of myself, but not at the expense of my family.

I have control over my health and wellness.

I will set aside preconceived notions about dieting.

APPENDIX

A two-week meal plan to help you live your best DADBOD.

WEEK 1
MONDAY

Breakfast—Sunrise Omelette:

- Heat up an egg pan, drop 1 tbsp butter in the pan, followed by 3 eggs
- Scramble the eggs in the pan and pour eggs onto the plate after cooking
- Add 3 ounces of diced broccoli and ½ ounce cheddar cheese

Snack—Greek Yogurt

Lunch—Burrito Bowl:

- Heat up a medium frying pan and add 1 tbsp butter
- Once hot, add 4 ounces of ground beef and brown the meat

- Once meat is brown, add 1 cup of mixed vegetables and mix until everything is hot
- Serve into a large bowl, add 1½ ounces of cheddar cheese and 1 tbsp sour cream

Snack—Protein Smoothie:

- Put 4–5 ice cubes in a blender, add 1 tablespoon of peanut butter, and a scoop of whey protein
- Add water for mixing and blend together

Dinner—Bunless Burgers:

- Cook 2 meat patties of ground beef, add a slice of cheese and either 1 ounce of ketchup or mustard
- Eat with a side of vegetables

TUESDAY

Breakfast—English Breakfast:

- Cook 4 turkey sausages, 2 eggs, and 3 slices of beefsteak tomato

Snack—Tuna and Spinach

Lunch—Grilled Chicken:

- Cook 2 chicken thighs, add a little bit of garlic and soy sauce with 3 ounces of broccoli

Snack—Protein Drink (low carb)

Dinner—Lamb Chops:

- Grill 2 lamb chops rubbed with barbecue sauce
- Cook about 5–6 ounces of red and yellow peppers, either grilled or pan-seared

WEDNESDAY

Breakfast—Protein Smoothie:

- Blend 2 scoops whey protein, 3 ounces of heavy whipping cream, 4–5 ice cubes, 1 tbsp of peanut butter

Snack—Beef Jerky (6 ounces)

Lunch—Avocado Bowl:

- Mix 1 avocado chopped with 4 ounces of shredded chicken, 1 ounce of shredded cheese, add salsa to taste

Snack—Mozzarella Cheese (4 ounces)

Dinner—Roasted Chicken Breast with Broccoli

THURSDAY

Breakfast—Bacon & Eggs:

- Cook 2 eggs however you'd like and 4 slices of bacon
- Add avocado if desired

Snack—Greek Yogurt

Lunch—Smoked Salmon:

- Serve 4–5 ounces of smoked salmon and 2 ounces of mozzarella cheese

Snack—Keto Bar

Dinner—Lamb Chops:

- Prepare 2 marinated lamb chops and a side of spinach and tomatoes, mix the vegetables with a little yogurt sauce

FRIDAY
Breakfast—Nut Bowl:

- Mix 2 tbsp peanut butter with 3 ounces of Greek yogurt

Snack—Protein Shake:

- Blend 2 scoops whey with 3 ounces of heavy whipping cream and ice cubes to taste

Lunch—Chicken Wings:

- Cook 8 chicken wings, serve with 4 celery stalks and side of ranch dressing

Snack—Protein Bar

Snack—String Cheese

Dinner—Fish Filet:

- Cook 4–5 ounces of fish (prefer halibut, but can do salmon) with 2 cups of salad and 4 ounces of asparagus

WEEK 2
MONDAY

Breakfast—Scrambled Eggs:

- Heat up an egg pan, drop 1 tbsp butter in the pan, followed by 3 eggs
- Scramble the eggs in the pan and pour eggs onto the plate after cooking
- Add ½ ounce cheddar cheese

Snack—Greek Yogurt

Lunch—Burgers:

- Heat up a medium frying pan and add 1 tbsp butter, once hot, add a pre-portioned hamburger patty (ground beef)
- Once cooked, add a layer of your favorite cheese on top
- Eat with a side of spinach and avocado

Snack—Sliced Turkey Rolled Up with Cream Cheese and Cucumber

Dinner—Stuffed Peppers:

- Stuff 2 large bell peppers with ground beef and top with cheddar cheese

- Can eat with hot sauce

TUESDAY

Breakfast—English Breakfast:

- Cook 4 turkey sausages, 2 eggs, 3 slices of beefsteak tomato

Snack—Tuna and Spinach Bowl

Lunch—Grilled Chicken:

- Cook 2 chicken thighs, add a little bit of garlic and soy sauce with 3 ounces of broccoli

Snack—Protein-Based Drink (low carb)

Dinner—Steak:

- Cook 6–8 ounces of red meat (steak) with a side of vegetables

WEDNESDAY

Breakfast—Protein Smoothie:

- Blend 2 scoops whey protein, 3 ounces of heavy whipping cream, 4–5 ice cubes, 1 tbsp of peanut butter

Snack—Peanut Butter (2 tablespoons)

Lunch—Avocado Bowl:

- Mix 1 avocado chopped with 4 ounces of shredded chicken, 1 ounce of shredded cheese, add salsa to taste

Snack—Beef Jerky

Dinner—Roasted Chicken Breast with Broccoli

THURSDAY

Breakfast—Bacon & Eggs:

- Cook 2 eggs however you'd like and 4 slices of bacon
- Add avocado if desired

Snack—Mozzarella Balls

Lunch—Smoked Salmon:

- Serve 4–5 ounces of smoked salmon and 2 ounces of mozzarella cheese

Snack—Protein Smoothie:

- Put about 4–5 ice cubes in a blender, add 1 tablespoon of peanut butter, and a scoop of whey protein
- Add water for mixing and blend together

Dinner—Chicken Sausage:

- Cook 6–8 ounces of chicken sausage topped with seared onions, and yellow and red peppers, with a side of asparagus

FRIDAY

Breakfast—Nut Bowl:

- Mix 2 tbsp peanut butter with 3 ounces of Greek yogurt

Snack—Protein Shake:

- Blend 2 scoops whey with 3 ounces of heavy whipping cream and ice cubes to taste

Lunch—Chicken Wings:

- Cook 8 chicken wings, serve with 4 celery stalks and side of ranch dressing

Snack—Protein Bar

Snack—Cheddar Cheese Squares

Dinner—Chicken Meatballs:

- Prepare 6–8 ounces of chicken meatballs topped with 2 ounces of parmesan cheese and a side of broccoli

ACKNOWLEDGMENTS

Just like fatherhood, writing this book was a journey; it took me a long time—years in fact—and I could not have done it without the support of my friends and family. All the times I asked you to read a chapter or two, or talk out an idea, a thought, or a situation, I cannot thank you enough. It means the world that you were there when I needed you.

To my wife, Dana, who was the first person I told I wanted to write a book about being a dad, and when I did, she said, "You should," not, "you're crazy." Thank you, my love.

To the team over at 7th Seal Advantage, Cherie Animashaun and Dr. Sheri Asuoha, you two showed me the way and turned DadBod into a real book. I am forever grateful and glad that I met you first.

To the publishing team at Scribe Media, who made this book not just something to read, but to hold in your hands. Katie, Rachael, Cristina, Caroline, Dylan, to name a few, thank you for making Dadbod come to life.

To my editor, Dave, you elevated this manuscript in ways that I did not think possible—you helped connect dots and thread the pages into the ideas I wanted to share—thank you.

To my parents, whom I would not be the man I am today without you—thank you.

To Mia, Eva, and Luca, this—like everything else I have to give—is for you.

To all the dads out there—I see you. Remember, we got here because we let ourselves, and we can dig ourselves out—and we will.

www.ingramcontent.com/pod-product-compliance
Lightning Source LLC
LaVergne TN
LVHW041612070526
838199LV00052B/3113